D1517200

FRED ROSENSTOCK

A Legend in Books & Art

Fred A. Rosenstock

FRED ROSENSTOCK

A Legend in Books & Art

By

DONALD E. BOWER

Foreword by Frank Waters

NORTHLAND PRESS

THIS VOLUME is based on research and interviews conducted by Dr. S. Lyman Tyler, Director, American West Center, University of Utah

ISBN 0-873580-149-0

Library of Congress Catalog Card Number 76-10419

Composed and Printed in the United States of America

To Frances Goodman Rosenstock, who shared Fred's ups and downs and said of him, "He isn't the best husband in the world, but life with him was never dull."

CONTENTS

ILLUSTRATIONS

FOREWORD

THE AUTHOR of this engrossing book cannot be suspected of having hidden under a table in the dining room of Denver's Brown Palace Hotel one evening not too long ago. Four of us were dining together: Jan Gartshore, the knowledgeable buyer for all the May-D&F bookstores in Colorado, Fred Rosenstock and his wife Frances, and I. It was an occasion for all of us. I had not seen Fred for some time, and this was the first evening that he and Frances had been out for months. Fred was a good storyteller. He held us entranced until closing time by recounting his experiences as a bookdealer from his arrival in Denver fifty years ago. I knew then we should have had a tape recorder to preserve his reminiscences. If Donald Bower was not tuned in on the floor at our feet, he might well have been. For he has recorded all the stories told us and a great deal more. He has written here Fred Rosenstock's complete biography from his childhood days in Austria.

This, in large measure, is a book about books — which offhand one might expect to be dull indeed. What makes it unusually appealing is one man's lifelong love of books, his uncanny nose for books, and his sleuth-like tracking of those rare, forgotten, or lost volumes that are now known and treasured Americana. It may be more than mere coincidence that Rosenstock's early collection activities marked the beginning of widespread interest in Western Americana, his specialty. Nor is it surprising that he acquired one of the largest collections in America and became acknowledged as a national authority on the books, writers, and hi-jinks of Western history. Not that this circumscribed his field of interest. He was interested in general Americana, and his Sherlock Holmes-style sleuthing took him over all the country.

Several other dealers and collectors I've known were interested in books only as marketable items to be priced according to their rarity, whether they were first editions or signed copies, the condition of their bindings, and so on. Rosenstock, on the contrary, read them all. He knew what they said, whether it was an original or a repetition of what had been written elsewhere.

Now books — let's admit it — are only about people and places. And a writer, by his art or the miracle of the written word, must somehow make the reader see, know, and *feel* the mysterious inner life of those he depicts. He can't fake it, however hard he tries, however glib he is. Otherwise we, the casual readers who know nothing about the subject, just as unaccountably lay the book aside and forget it.

It seems to me that the real validity and the only true function of a collector, as of a critic (few of which exist today), is to discern out of the overwhelming flood of books those which mirror the evanescent quality of their moment of truth. He resurrects from the past, and perpetuates for the future, those few assertions of time and place out of the multitude of the commonplace. To separate this grain from the chaff requires of course an artist in his own right, a man who knows not only books but the diverse aspects of life itself.

Rosenstock, as Bower amply shows, was such a man. A man with such poor eyesight he wore glasses from the age of ten. And incidentally it was this that brought him to Denver. Traveling from Washington, D.C., to California, where he intended to settle because of ill health, he lost his only pair of glasses on the train and was obliged to stop over in Denver for a new pair — a stopover that has lasted for a half-century. Despite this handicap, Rosenstock was a lover of sports, a tennis, baseball, football, and boxing fan, and attended the theater regularly. Devoted to his family, he still traveled constantly to every part of the country on buying trips, meeting people in every walk of life. Bower relates countless stories of his intimate associations with them. All of these interests were grist to his mill. He was foremost and always a collector.

None of us know what mysterious forces make us what we are. Yet I have often wondered just what inherent predispositions and influences enabled a small boy in a remote little hamlet in the Carpathian mountains of central Europe to learn Yiddish, Ruthenian, Polish, and German, and to read English at the age of seven; to sell in America his first book, one he'd bought for twenty cents and sold for five dollars; and to become a leading collector and authority on Western Americana. Perhaps it was simply that instilled generations of Old World culture helped him to see the raw New World in clear perspective.

Certainly Denver in the twenties was the place to see Western Americana still in the making. The town was the focal center of the entire Rocky Mountain West. I remember it well as it was then, when Rosenstock opened his Denver Book Shop on Stout Street in 1922, followed by his Bargain Book Store on Fifteenth Street, in 1928. This area — between Seventeenth and Fifteenth streets, on Curtis, Champa, and Arapahoe — was the heart of the city's life. Curtis was the great White Way, lined with movie palaces featuring films of Marion Davies. Down the street was Baur's sweet-tooth emporium where we used to take our best girls for an ice-cream soda. Through the lobby of the historic Windsor Hotel walked fabulous old-timers. As Bower so accurately records, white-gowned Aimee Semple McPherson packed the auditorium with her perfervid sermons, but I remember she was not averse to haranguing a crowd on the street corner. Hop Alley was no longer a rendezvous for opium smokers, but it still boasted thievery, murder, and suicide. Farther east rose the majestic Brown Palace to which my father and grandfather took us for the annual conventions of stockmen and miners. And everywhere were small secondhand bookstores — like the Bargain Book Store — where we could buy books for fifty cents apiece.

I did not meet Rosenstock until about 1950 or 1951 when he came to Albuquerque with his daughter. I asked him then, rather naively, why he was so hell-bent on collecting all such stuff about the West, its history, books, and writers. "Frank," he told me, "this is the essence of Western

America, of a new country's beliefs and customs. A grass-roots literature. You unconsciously appreciate it yourself. Keep at it!"

How acute, how true he was! In the many years since, he has collected my own books with those of countless other writers, past and present. Plagued with inquiries as to where one might obtain a rare book, a first edition, I've always had a stock answer. "See Fred Rosenstock in Denver. He'll get it for you."

Fred of course was a Pirate, a Scrooge who bought cheap and sold dear. One day I walked into his store with a wary director of a California museum who wanted to pick up an out-of-print book. He selected from the stacks a few nonessential items and then casually asked Fred for the particular book he wanted. "Hmm," replied Fred just as casually. "I'll look around to see if I happen to have a copy. Why don't you come back tomorrow?" That evening he went to his back storeroom or wherever he kept his rarer books and brought out one of a dozen copies he had obtained. But he was just as generous. For years he kept contributing precious collections of all kinds to universities, libraries, and state archives.

Someone has written that a man is no greater than his biographer. Don Bower measures up to his task. He sets Rosenstock in proper perspective against the phases of history — World War I and II, the mass migrations from Europe to America, the Great Depression — which were his backgrounds. These broad strokes on a large canvas are matched by Bower's meticulous attention to detail. His outstanding biography traces Rosenstock's continually expanding activities from book collecting to publishing books under his own imprint; and his long growing interest in collecting Western paintings, leading to his present plans, at the age of eighty, to open an art gallery. As a result we read here, for perhaps the first time, the full life of a unique bookman who has contributed so much to our preservation and appreciation of our own unique American literature and art.

FRANK WATERS

PREFACE

IT IS DIFFICULT TO IMAGINE what kind of a world it might have been if there had not been an Einstein or an Edison, a Columbus or a Curie, a Churchill or a Lincoln. These were people who were changers of the world.

During the past several years, I have become a close friend of a man who has been a world-changer in the area of Western Americana, Fred Asher Rosenstock. At my first meeting, I admit I was a bit uneasy, somewhat awed by his reputation and overwhelmed by his knowledge of rare books and art of the West. He seemed, as I stood in the wide aisle between the high stacks of rare treasures, to be preoccupied, his face grim, his eyes piercing. But after I had explained my purpose — I was looking for a Russell painting to illustrate a magazine article — his eyes took on a sparkle, the grimness gave way to a smile, and he began to tell me the story of how he first started to acquire Russells.

More than five years later, by which time I considered myself friend, customer, and a Rosenstock-addict, I had the opportunity to become his confidante and biographer. One of the fortunate side-effects of writing this book has been the knowledge I gained, not only about the man, but about that entire arena of Western Americana — rare books, art, biblio-philes, collectors.

Such a book — about such a man — could not have been written without help from many sources. In more than eighty years of an active life, Fred Rosenstock's career has involved an extensive and diverse cir-cle of people: authors, editors, scholars, artists, librarians, book sellers and scouts, historians, collectors, museum curators. I have met, talked to and corresponded with dozens of these Rosenstock acquaintances and owe more debts of gratitude than I can ever repay.

Without question, the single person — excluding Fred himself — who provided the most valuable information was Dr. S. Lyman Tyler, presently the Director of the American West Center at the University of Utah, and a longtime close friend of the Rosenstocks. For six years Lyman Tyler devoted much of his time interviewing Fred, taping perhaps a hundred hours of formal and informal conversations, in researching facts about Fred's early life, in producing extensive notes about his business, his friends, his family. Unselfishly Lyman has made available to me all of the material he had accumulated, and without this kind of help this book would not have been possible.

Many of Fred's companions in the Denver Posse of The Westerners were invaluable in providing anecdotes and a personal insight into the Rosenstock personality. Some of these friends were Fred Mazzulla, Dabney Otis Collins, and Dr. Nolie Mumey.

Dr. Nelson Goodman of Denver was not only an important aid during the early days of the Rosenstock Bargain Book Store, but also provided important facts concerning the operation of the business that might otherwise have been lost.

Special thanks must be given to Harold S. Lindbloom, Fred's one-time partner in the school book business; Velma Linford, a vanguard Wyoming educator and an Old West Publishing Company author; Alys Freeze, former head of the Western History Department of the Denver Public Library; James Parsons, art connoisseur; Dean Krakel, director of the National Cowboy Hall of Fame; David Lavender, historian *par excellence*; the late Lester Gehman; Dr. James Sandoe, Special Collections Librarian at the University of Colorado; Mitchell A. Wilder, Director of the Amon Carter Museum in Fort Worth, Texas; Fred Rosenstock's daughter, Marilyn Weiker; Dr. Philip W. Whiteley; Sam Weller; Melvin W. Schoberlin; Kenneth Sender; Edith Permut; and Steve Good, Fred's knowledgeable assistant who offered numerous suggestions concerning the manuscript. The care taken by Paul Weaver and his staff at Northland Press is also appreciated.

I also wish to thank the following authors and publishers for permitting use of material from their books: Robert L. Perkin, *The First Hundred Years* (Doubleday, 1954); Rufus Learsi, *The Jews in America* (World Publishing Co., 1954); John T. Winterich, *Collector's Choice* (Greenberg, New York, 1928); A. S. W. Rosenbach, *Books and Bidders* (Little Brown and Co., 1927).

DONALD E. BOWER

CHAPTER I

MILE-HIGH DENVER

IT WAS A SATURDAY AFTERNOON, and the young Jewish immigrant was wandering through the business district of Rochester, New York, but with an objective in mind. He saw the sign, "Second Hand Books," and crossed the street, walked into the musty building.

Books were piled in heaps on large tables, others askew on the floor, some on shelves extending the length of the store. He peered through thick-lensed glasses, occasionally picking up a dusty volume and leafing through it. The proprietor merely observed the browsing high school student, convinced by the boy's shabby appearance that he was not much of a prospective customer.

For almost an hour the boy remained, finally selecting a slim, very worn volume entitled, *Niagara Falls,* with a number of old woodcut illustrations depicting this great wonder of the world as it appeared to the first white men. The proprietor agreed to sell it for twenty cents, and the young boy fished into his pocket, felt for the single twenty-five cent coin, made the transaction. He had only a nickel left out of his week's allowance, but in his hand he had a treasure, and he left the story buoyant both in step and spirit.

The boy was Fred Asher Rosenstock, and the year was 1913. He was excited over his purchase and rushed back to his modest home at 19 Leopold Street. He pulled a sheet of paper from his high school notebook, and wrote a letter to the public library at Niagara Falls, describing in detail the book he had purchased and suggesting that it might be something the library would want.

Ten days later he received a letter from the librarian, advising that they wanted the volume and would pay five dollars for it. Many years would pass before Fred Rosenstock would make another sale, but the spark ignited that day would never die.

On November 30, 1949, another spark ignited that almost extinguished the career of Fred Rosenstock, who had become one of the most noted rare book dealers in the West. As was his habit he was working late in his store, the Bargain Book Store in downtown Denver, Colorado, discussing some rare volumes with a prospective customer.

"First we could smell the faint odor of smoke, then I heard some crackling sounds. I called the fire department, and my friend and I were investigating when the first trucks arrived."

As reported in the *Rocky Mountain News,* December 1, 1949: "When firemen arrived, they found little flame, but exceptionally heavy smoke which clung to the ground. As they entered the burning store, five members of Rescue Squad No. Four were immediately felled by the fumes. Another fireman succumbed to the smoke at 11:15 P.M."

At the height of the excitement, Fred remembered that he had placed a painting by Charles Russell, worth several thousand dollars, in one of the basement storage bins. As soon as the firemen would let him in, he borrowed a pair of their hip boots and waded toward the area, filled with trepidation. Fortunately the level of the water was a few inches below the bin that held the Russell.

Total damage to the Bargain Book Store and neighboring businesses was estimated at $100,000, and Fred recovered $25,000 from his insurance company. As so often happens, damage from the smoke and water was greater than from the actual fire. The greatest losses were to books stored in the basement, which were under two feet of water. Friends, relatives, well-wishers came to his aid, bringing scoop shovels, buckets, and trucks to clean up the mess and salvage a few of the volumes that had not come completely unglued.

A book, to Fred Rosenstock, was almost like a living thing, and should a customer accidentally drop a volume, he would grimace in pain as though he himself had just dropped from the customer's hands. The fire had a traumatic effect on Fred, as revealed in this letter to Walter McCausland a year later: "This fire didn't help me physically or mentally. For a few weeks after, I was so knocked out by what happened that I felt sure I wouldn't continue in business, but just sell out what was left and forget it. Then, gradually, I changed my mind and decided to go on. The owners of the building rebuilt and made a beautiful new front (at more rent, naturally), and we have an additional room which we are slowly making into a rare book room; also, we have a fairly long lease (five years) which we did not have before."

Between 1913, the year when he accomplished his first transaction in bookselling, and 1949, when his bookstore was virtually demolished, Fred survived two world wars, the great depression, severe personal illness, a failure in his first bookstore venture, and some extreme losses at the hands of auctioneers. Fortunately for the student of Western history, the scholar, the writer, and the buff, he had the desire and determination to seek out and preserve as a part of the American heritage thousands of old and rare volumes, manuscripts, journals, maps, and illustrations that might otherwise have been forever lost.

From his days as a child in Biala Potok, his small hometown in Austria, he had shown an interest in books, developing reading skills and comprehension at an early age. Whether in Czernowitz, Rochester, Washington, or Denver, many of his hours were spent searching through the piles of books and stacks in bookstores, and long before he had seriously thought of becoming a dealer or collector he had accumulated a respectable collection of first editions and other rare volumes.

Fred, like many Jewish people, has been a devout believer in miracles, convinced that many of the significant events in his life occurred as the result of some supernatural accident. He might have attributed his eventual start as a bookseller to one of his so-called miracles, but more realistically it might have been attributed to a gust of wind.

He had spent the World War I years in Washington, D.C., but following the Armistice, his eventual release from the Army, and almost two years of employment with an outdoor sign company, his health began to fail and his doctor ordered him to move to the West.

It was typical of Fred Rosenstock that his feelings of regret at leaving Washington, his family, his friends, were tempered by his excitement concerning the future, his enthusiastic quest for a new adventure. And when he recalled the doctor's admonition to leave Washington for the sake of good health and a long life, he shed no tears as the train chugged its way out of Union Station.

Traveling by train in the early twenties, especially in the summertime, was not particularly comfortable, but it was, for all practical purposes, the only way to go. Air-conditioned Pullman cars didn't arrive until the late thirties, and prior to that passengers had a choice of sweltering in a closed railroad car or opening the windows and suffering the smoke, soot, and cinders from the locomotive stacks.

"I had decided even before I left Washington to go all the way West — to California. My employers were good to me. They wanted me to get well, and, hopefully, to eventually return to them. They offered to pay my travel and medical expenses for six months, and did."

Following a brief layover and a change of trains in Chicago, the young Rosenstock boarded the Chicago and Northwestern. "It was a very warm day in August, and as we went west through Illinois and Iowa, it was even hotter. Finally, after Des Moines, I decided to try to get some respite from the soot and cinders inside, and went to the observation car. I was sitting outside, on the platform, absorbed in a magazine. I was wearing 'pincer' glasses, which hooked on the nose, without frames. I was not aware that the glasses were not properly adjusted on my nose; they were slightly loose, in fact. As the shadows began to lengthen in the late afternoon, a little wind rose up, and all of a sudden, without warning, a gusty breeze literally blew my glasses off into the void with the train going at full speed.

"The loss of my glasses presented a severe problem. First of all, I am nearsighted and have worn glasses since I was ten. Without them I would not be able to see the distant scenery — and this, for me, would be losing a major pleasure of the trip. I hailed the conductor, told him of my mishap, and asked him where I could get off to have some new glasses fitted." The conductor suggested Omaha, which would be the next stop. Whether it was the name of the city, some intuitive notion, or the fact that the young traveler had tired of watching mile after mile of rolling cornfields, he vetoed the idea of getting off at Omaha. Querying the trainman further, he learned that the next major city, some five hundred miles west, was Denver.

"At once there flickered through my mind some images of Denver which had collected in me, an Easterner, over the years. Buffalo Bill! Gold! Rocky Mountains! I said to myself, 'That's where I'll get off.'"

Even in the early twenties, Denver had achieved significant status among the cities of the West. Population-wise, it had grown in four decades from a frontier town of 34,555 to a metropolis of over 200,000. Denver, the "Mile-High" city, had its origin in 1858 at the junction of the South Platte River and Cherry Creek, "where the mountains meet the plains," and by 1920 sprawled for miles along the foothills of the snow-capped Front Range of the Rockies. A beautiful city, with a magnificent backdrop, it became the economic, cultural and governmental center of the entire Rocky Mountain West.

The train pulled into Denver early the next morning, and the weather was cool and clear, with a deep blue sky framing the rugged peaks to the west. "I stepped out of the Union Depot — at that time an almost unbelievably busy place — and lo and behold! — I felt like a new man. After an inquiry, I began to walk toward the downtown area. I amazed myself by the sudden buoyancy I seemed to have while walking the ten blocks to Sixteenth and Champa streets, whereas in Washington I could hardly walk a block without becoming completely fagged out."

Fred was impressed by everything he saw, particularly at the 330-foot Daniels and Fisher's Tower, a somewhat inaccurate replica of the campanile in Venice, but still a distinctive landmark; and by the gold-domed capitol building overlooking the downtown business district.

"I walked into the first optical store that met my eyes. The man promised to have new glasses for me the very next day. And he was as good as his word. I had my glasses the next day, and there was no reason why I couldn't continue my trip to California. But I didn't rush back to Union Station. I'd always been a baseball fan, and I read in the paper about a ball game. It was being played at Merchants' Park, on South Broadway, near the big Montgomery Ward store — it's a shopping center now. I'd had lots of experience seeing major league ball at Griffith Park in Washington, but I wanted to see how baseball was played in the Western League. I enjoyed the game and at its end surprised myself by a sudden yearning for food — a good steak, if you please — the first such desire I had experienced in many weeks.

"Denver at that time had many fine restaurants. I strolled into one — it was Watrous' Restaurant — ordered steak, and it was delicious! As I waited, my eyes wandered and centered their attention on a beautiful large oil painting that hung on the wall and appeared to be the showpiece of the place. I wasn't seriously interested in art at that time, but even as I ate, I continued to be fascinated by this painting — which vividly depicted a scene during the Indian wars of the Custer period. The memory of this painting never left me, and I think, even then, that I knew someday I would have to have it."

It was Fred's intent, initially, to continue on to California, but as the hours passed he became more reticent about leaving. The days were mild, the climate dry, the skies blue, and the air clean. He had his glasses and his ticket for California; the only excuse for not continuing his journey was his sudden love affair with the Mile-High City. "On my third day," he recalls, "I did something that was my habit wherever I lived — in the days of my youth in Rochester, and later in Washington — and that was to visit the secondhand bookstores. In those days I wasn't looking for books to sell — I really read books (and I still do), and not exclusively books of history. My range was wide, although history predominated. The downtown area of Denver supported at least half a dozen bookstores dealing in used books. They could afford the low rents of that time, whereas now they are shunted off to remote areas — homes, barns, anything. I wound up buying about as many books as I could carry, and was delighted to find the bookmen so genial and amiable that I knew I would be at home in their circle.

"A few more pleasant days in Denver and I began to ponder the wisdom of going to California. I sensed I was responding to the better climate. In fact, everything about Denver in that short week contributed to my decision to stay."

Following World War I Fred had been employed in Washington as a sales representative for an outdoor advertising firm, the Cusack Company, which had agreed to pay his expenses to the West Coast. Once young Rosenstock was certain he would be staying in Denver, he wrote John Shoemaker, the branch manager at Cusack, advising him of this change in plans and also asking if he could recommend a doctor in the Mile-High City.

"I was referred to Dr. E. A. Peterson. He turned out to be a friendly, capable physician, and upon hearing my story and examining me, said the change of climate wasn't enough." He immediately arranged for Fred to move out of the hotel into a private home several miles east of downtown, near the site of present-day Stapleton International Airport. "I was there for about a month, and I used to walk to Colfax Avenue and take the trolley to my favorite haunts, the bookstores, just to get away."

Dr. Peterson eventually arranged for Fred to stay at the Oakes Rest Home (now a Catholic convent), "where I could get lots of rest and good food. This was a first class institution sponsored and operated by a religious organization and directed by the Rev. Frederick Oakes, a fine administrator (although a bit pompous and straightlaced). There were approximately a hundred patients there — some only slightly ill, and a few that seemed to be not sick at all."

For a young man with enthusiasm, talent, a lust for adventure and a determination to achieve some kind of success in this world, his restful days in the convalescent home became tiresome, "and time began to be heavy on my hands. I knew it was good for me to rest, but I was feeling better and my energy was increasing. There were several other men in a similar condition — ordered to rest, but not really incapacitated, and we discovered a mutual interest — playing poker.

"It happened that my room was quite spacious, and so there it was that the game was held nearly every afternoon. It was a friendly game, and actually I was not a winner, but it happened that a few amateurs who really had no business in the game dropped a few shekels and it got back to Reverend Oakes that a gambling operation was going on in his very respectable domain, and in my room! So I got a call to see him in his office. After asking me myriad questions, he absolved me from 'running a game' but said it had to stop. It did."

From his days as a child, Fred was friendly, gregarious, and soon was acquainted with most of the patients at Oakes home. One of the other residents at that time was Temple Buell, a wealthy Denverite and socialite-philanthropist. In the late 1960s he made a substantial contribution to Colorado Women's College and for a time the institution was officially known as Temple Buell College. "I never knew why Temple Buell was there — he seemed *extra* healthy to me and I liked him very much, particularly his joviality. He had a Ford — a 'tin Lizzy' — as I recall, and once or twice I accompanied him on little jaunts with friends, and not always men. There was no hard and fast rule about getting *out* of the Home in the evening, but you had to be back by ten to get in. Once I was late, but by pre-arrangement, I tapped on the window of a young lady resident (who had become a good friend) and she let me in through her window."

Fred had been endowed not only with an outgoing friendliness, but with a spirit of helpfulness, and occasionally — throughout his life — these seemingly admirable characteristics led him into difficulty. "My doctor, Dr. Peterson, would come to see me twice a week, and he thought I was doing fine. Other residents or patients who had their own doctors, and particularly some who weren't doing so well, observed my rather amazing and rapid improvement and asked who was treating me.

Naturally, I was able to speak of Dr. Peterson with enthusiasm, with the result that several of my new-made friends said, 'When your doctor calls to see you, please bring him to me. I would like to see him.' It did not strike me as unethical at the time, and, wonder of wonders, soon my doctor was 'making the rounds' like the mailman. Almost overnight he had acquired ten or twelve 'customers.'

"I felt genuinely happy for them and for my doctor, and it never did occur to me that I had unintentionally done a selling job. Of course what was happening was that other doctors were losing patients. One doctor in particular was badly hurt — he lost three. Once more I was called to Rev. Oakes's office. He asked, 'Rosenstock, are you *really* sick or are you a hired plant for an unprofessional doctor?' Then he told me that several of the affected doctors had complained and threatened to discontinue sending patients to the home. I hotly denied the allegations and wound up by saying, 'Reverend Oakes, I won't be a thorn to you much longer. I am feeling much better and I'm going to look for a job.' "

Except for the plague of inflation, the post–World War I period in the United States was prosperous, particularly in the urban areas. Automobile sales were soaring, employment reached peacetime heights, and the Roaring Twenties — in spite of Prohibition — seemed destined to become known as America's Golden Era. Politically, the tenor of the times developed into one of conservatism and isolation. After all, the "war to end war" had been fought and won, the world was now "safe for democracy," and the people of this great land were ready to build a fence around its borders. Even the over-publicized, unwarranted Red Scare of 1919–1920 failed to engender any lasting fears in the hearts of average Americans. A new version of the post–Civil War Ku Klux Klan had risen again in the South, and by 1919 over a hundred thousand of the white-sheeted bigots were harassing Negroes, Jews, Catholics, and symbolic crosses were being burned on hillsides.

In Denver, the skyrocketing population boom of the previous three decades had temporarily subsided. Seventeenth Street had become the financial center of the Rocky Mountain West, and the Equitable Building at Seventeenth and Stout, reaching six stories into the western sky, was the tallest office edifice in the Mile-High city. While the historic Windsor Hotel was beginning to tire, it still retained much of its original grandeur and some of Denver's notable visitors were occasionally seen in its lobby.

"It was a time," wrote John P. Lewis, one-time reporter for the *Rocky Mountain News,* "touched by the joyous insanities of prohibition, and those who survived it look back with nostalgia, I think, to the days of the speakeasy. It was a time touched by cancerous, fearful hatreds and intolerances. The Ku Kluxers all but controlled the state for a time. There were mobs and violence. Black Jack Jerome's strikebreakers were kicked into bloody insensibility in their overturned street cars at the very doors of the Cathedral before the federal troops restored order. It was a time of corruption. Nationally, the Harding regime came and went. Locally, police protection made Denver the home of America's finest confidence men until District Attorney Philip S. Van Cise brought in outside police and broke it up, meanwhile giving heart failure to all the owners of all the whorehouses in Denver by publicly measuring their properties for closing by way of conning the conmen into thinking he was after prostitutes, not thieves.

"There was a mystic side to the times. White-gowned Aimee Semple McPherson packed the auditorium with listeners and cluttered the wings with canes and crutches of the healed, some of whom went back to retrieve them next day. The House of David brought enlightenment to Arapahoe Street, and Jim Goodheart did his good works for the poor devils in the gutter until he stumbled and backslid himself.

"There was violence, crime, murder, suicide — whatever else was missed, we on the papers were intent about that and never let human tragedy slip by unheralded. There was thievery and incompetence in some of the banks, and long years before the national crash of '29, Denver had its own series of reverberating financial failures.

"And there was vision. They were presumptuous, perhaps, but some people saw the growth that has since come about. The Moffat Tunnel was built, and water brought under the Divide and the Civic Center nurtured and developed at a time when most cities were building toward new slums and congestion. In the twenties, Denver had sort of an itch to be better than it was. . . .”

This was the Denver in which Fred Rosenstock found himself after leaving the Oakes Home in February, 1921. “I had no difficulty,” he says, “finding a job. As a matter of fact, I went to work for a billboard concern in Denver called the Curran Company, actually an affiliate of my Washington employer. The owner, old Jim Curran, had started many years before as a billposter and made a lot of money in outdoor advertising and other pursuits.

“The man at the head of the sales department was Tracy Reeve, a man of character and culture for whom I formed a great affection. Reeve’s father, quite an elderly man at that time, was also in the office as a bookkeeper. I spent many pleasant hours in his home becoming acquainted with his fine collection of Americana.

“I began to earn and save a little money, and soon considered myself a confirmed Coloradoan. I knew this would be *my* country.” By early summer, however, Fred had become disenchanted with James Curran. “It struck him that if you had not started as a billposter you were some sort of interloper, and things in general were getting unsavory. My good friend Tracy Reeve — my immediate boss — seemed to feel the same way although, as it turned out, he stayed with Curran for several years more.”

One reason, undoubtedly, for his dissatisfaction with Curran had little relationship to the man. Fred had observed his own father, Abraham, spending his life as a garment worker and a tailor, when the elder Rosenstock’s true love was in the role of a scholar. And Fred’s heart was firmly pressed between the pages of a musty first edition. At age twenty-six, he didn’t visualize that he would own a bookstore, perhaps, but he was certain that he would be a book collector. It was time to burn the bridges of boredom that he felt in the outdoor advertising business, and to start pursuing his ambitions. “I began to grow tired and frustrated at grinding it out by myself, and at the same time my parents and sister, still in Washington, became lonesome for me." In August, 1921, he wrote to his parents and asked them to join him. "My father disposed of his small business, and my family came to Denver. I found a little house to rent at 2711 Gilpin Street, and paid eight months' rent in advance — about thirty-five dollars a month — and the family arrived and we were reunited. Life took on a new dimension."

The conscientious Rosenstock, feeling a sense of obligation to his former employers in Washington for all they had done for him, remained with Curran until the end of 1921, knowing, however, that he would soon be trying his wings in the book business. Those last few months of 1921, in Fred's words, "I began to haunt the bookshops. To give you a picture of what I observed then: there was a big downtown new bookstore. Their lines were actually more extensive than they are today. In addition to popular books, there were fine sets in beautiful bindings. One book section in a department store had, surprisingly, a fine and extensive section of French books — in French. Just imagine! To think that fifty years ago the trade would support a line of French books.

"Another store dabbled a little in reference books — dictionaries, almanacs, Bibles, diaries. But my real love was the secondhand stores. At that time, the busiest part of downtown Denver was between Fifteenth and Seventeenth streets, on Champa, Curtis, and Arapahoe. There were several used book stores, one on Fifteenth Street between Arapahoe and Lawrence. What halcyon days I had there! There was a very extensive fiction collection, which I visited regularly once I began to learn a little bit about first editions and collectors' items. Everything was fifty cents, and I found some excellent buys!

"Another secondhand store kept its books immaculately clean. I adopted this practice myself later on when I went into business. Every secondhand book that would come in would get a cleaning up so that they just shone on the shelves.

"Then there was a little store on Fourteenth near the present-day telephone building. It was pretty progressive. So far as I can recall they were the first dealers to pay attention to first editions and collectors' items. In fact, they had a book about first editions — and I didn't know up to that time that such a book had ever been published.

"And there was a sort of a chain operation, a new and used bookstore run by Roy Adair. Roy's father had been in the secondhand book business in Minneapolis for many years. He sent Roy to Denver to open up a branch. Old man Adair was sort of the skinflint of the Denver book trade. He would come to Roy's store quite often and hover around the register to make sure everything went in. He may have missed some of the flow. It was amusing, watching him walk around with one hand in his pocket, jingling money. But he really knew quite a little about Western Americana and had even issued a catalog or two from his Minneapolis store.

"Those were glorious days. Denver had not yet launched its '500,000 by 1930' campaign. It was safe to walk the streets at any hour, day or night. During that period I got initiated into a poker game circle, a nice respectable one. It was mostly booksellers, and even though I wasn't yet in the business, they welcomed me as a sort of kindred soul. Most of the time we played in the very basement of the store which I eventually owned at Fifteenth and Tremont. Sanford Lockard was the host, and we were never raided. But about Denver being safe — I remember many the night I walked home all the way from Fifteenth to Twenty-seventh and Gilpin, some two miles. I was often broke and had to walk. Besides, the night air was invigorating and I did some heavy thinking along the way; moreover, it was a form of penance to walk."

It was a predestined fact in Fred Rosenstock's life that he would become a book dealer. In 1925 his Uncle Morris Ashenberg, referring to Fred's interest in books, wrote: "I claim that you was initiated in this work when you was a small kid through my books I used to buy when I could spare. But unfortunately I never had money enough." Grandmother Ashenberg also nurtured his interest in books and learning. In the same letter, Morris continued: "I delivered your message and your gift of money to my mother. I had read for her your letter, also the account of your collection of books. How happy it made her. Like the artist who sees his dream realized and expressed on canvas or in clay in its full glory, so she sees you — an expression of her dreams — to see her offspring getting an education.

"When we were small, when hunger, cold, and starvation were our constant companions, these things didn't concern her at all. To get for us a worldly education, this was her passion. And this ideal keeps her alive now, when she sees her grandchildren, every one of them, making good in this field."

To Fred's parents, his interest in books was related to this drive for education; an ingredient so necessary to achievement, and to a full life in the world they knew. In America, somehow, all this was possible. His sister Anne expressed her view of his interests as a youth: "Whenever he had a nickel or a dime for spending money, he would browse around the Salvation Army and pick up books that he thought were interesting, usually relating to history or the life of some historical character."

From January to March of 1922, no longer hampered by his job with Curran, Fred devoted his time to book-searching, and perhaps some soul-searching as well. Finally, as spring came to the Rockies, he found a store at 1758 Stout Street, and opened The Denver Book Shop. At that moment, fraught with excitement, Fred Rosenstock was convinced that he had fulfilled his destiny. He was yet to discover that one's destiny can be an elusive pinnacle.

CHAPTER II

A NOBLE EXPERIMENT

TO FRED ROSENSTOCK, 1922 was a year of promises. He had laid his plans for the future, and if he anticipated any difficulties they were that his enthusiasm and impatience would overrule his sound business judgment. His personal book collection had developed impressively, but he realized that to be successful as a book dealer he would have to accumulate not only a larger stock, but volumes that could not be found on every bookseller's shelf.

From childhood days to the present Fred has been a devout believer in miracles — not a unique doctrine among Jews, many of whom are convinced it is a miracle that Jewry has survived the persecution and mass annihilations over the ages. Hoping to open his store by the first of March of 1922, Fred devoted his time to seeking out collections. "I advertised in the papers in Denver and Colorado Springs, and I was lucky. There were lots of wealthy families in the Springs, many with fine books, and one who answered my ad was the widow of Charles T. Wilder, who had been the editor of the Colorado Springs *Gazette*. She had about two thousand books, some of them excellent, and all in good condition. I didn't have much money, but I really wanted the collection. I don't know if it was my smile, or the fact that I was a young man trying to get started in business, but she took a liking to me and let me have the library with the wonderful provision that I could pay for it a little at a time."

This marked the beginning of a relationship that has continued for half a century. "I was about eleven when Fred came to our house,"

Charles T. Wilder, Jr., recalls, "and I remember that smile of his. My mother liked him instantly, and really wanted to help." Mitchell, the younger son, eventually became the director of the Amon Carter Museum of Western Art in Fort Worth, Texas. "He is still one of my intimate friends," Fred emphasizes, "and our relationship is especially close because of his position at Amon Carter."

Another "miracle," or at the least another lucky purchase Fred made at that time involved the private library of a prominent Denver businessman, Henry S. Winans. Fred recalls, "This was a collection wide-ranging in subject matter, about fifteen hundred books, and all in pristine condition. I also acquired some fine sectional bookcases which today are prized as rare antiques. Here, once again, I must have impressed him with my earnestness of purpose, for not only did he let me have the library but agreed to let me pay for them as I sold them."

In the early twenties the best bookstore in Colorado Springs was Grimwoods. They dealt in new books, and had been in business since the late nineteenth century. "Mr. Grimwood had died," Fred notes, "and I went to the store one day and talked to his widow. Of course I wasn't interested in new books, but I thought she might have some first editions or something stuck away from the early days. Suddenly I saw a light in her eyes. 'I have some things in the basement,' she told me, 'left-overs from end-of-the-year book sales of the past thirty years.'"

When she showed him the basement, Fred was elated. "I spent three hours there, and ended up buying about fifteen hundred books. It was a windfall. As an example, there were about ten two-volume sets — boxed and in pristine condition — of *The Life and Times of Audubon,* by Herrick. Today they would be worth at least fifty or sixty dollars a set."

As a result of one of his advertisements in the Denver papers, Fred also obtained several thousand books from the Andrew S. Hughes library. Hughes was an early pioneer attorney in Central City and Denver and progenitor of the Hughes family, which remains as an influential factor in the Rocky Mountain region of today. "Again," Fred says, "I was lucky. Not only were the volumes in excellent condition, replete with Coloradana, but they, too, let me pay for the collection over a period of time."

These were exciting and productive moments. Fred, when concentrating on the purchase of books, was at his best. For a young man born in virtual poverty, who emigrated to a strange land when only nine, he had visions of following in the footsteps of Horatio Alger. His engaging smile, his enthusiasm, and his openness and honesty combined with an astute knowledge of the world of books were all elements that should have led him to instant success.

But he was to learn that buying books was only one-half of succeeding in the bookstore business. The other half was selling them. Unfortunately, as events were eventually to prove, the location Fred selected for his first store was not the best. Most of the activity in the early twenties was centered around Sixteenth Street and Champa, Curtis, and Arapahoe. Fred had found a vacant store at 1758 Stout Street, close to Eighteenth, and several blocks away from the traffic flow. He had certain misgivings at the time, but these were overshadowed by his impatience to fulfill his life's dream.

On March 1, 1922, the Denver Book Shop opened for business. "At first I didn't specialize in Western Americana. It was an antiquarian book store, offering rare and out-of-print books, fine bindings, sets of books, first editions." There probably was a gasp of surprise among Fred Rosenstock's poker-playing partners when the Denver Book Shop came on the scene, for the young entrepreneur had been quietly buying collections, saying nothing of his planned venture to his bookmen-friends. "I soon had several thousand volumes, but I was pretty naive at that point about the bookstore business, even though I was a knowledgeable collector. I was learning the business from day to day, often painfully.

"For instance, I acquired a lot of books that included a copy of the rare Wilhelm and Wharton *History and Directory of Denver,* the original 1866 edition, with a value even then of at least $150. The next day I traded it off to another dealer for a few dollars worth of books on engineering just because I had recently had a call for such books.

"Once, in a small, private library, I acquired a first edition of *Cabbages and Kings* by O. Henry, in pristine condition, in the original jacket. Shortly after a man walked into the store and asked about O. Henry items. When I showed him this volume, his eagerness made me hesitate. I asked him to come back after I had a chance to 'look it up.'

"Actually, I didn't have anything to look it up in, but ran over to a bookseller friend for advice. He said, 'Don't take less than five dollars — it's a collector's item.' Actually, it was then appearing in catalogs for from fifty to sixty dollars.

"When the customer returned the next day, I asked for the five dollars with my heart in my mouth, and got it. This was one of my better individual sales to that time. It wasn't long until I began to become better acquainted with that unique tribe called 'collectors,' and soon learned that first editions had special values, and that there were various 'points' — just like in judging thoroughbreds — that helped identify first editions."

Early in the twentieth century the competition for rare books and research collections intensified, not only between dealers and private collectors, but even more so between dealers and educational libraries. One example of an extensive library that could have been a bonanza had it been made available to the competitive marketplace was Hubert Howe Bancroft's in San Francisco, which ultimately was purchased for a comparatively nominal sum by the University of California at Berkeley.

It is natural that some bookmen resent this growing tendency for important collections to be purchased by, or sometimes donated to, various institutions. The preface to the McClurg (Chicago) catalog published in November of 1912 states: "The growing scarcity of early books is not due to purchases by collectors of rare books alone, though there are many such collectors. The subject is one which appeals strongly to the great class of readers who are interested in our history, and this interest is genuine, growing as opportunities for study are offered.

"The result has been that not only individuals but all institutions of learning, public and school libraries, historical societies, university libraries, etc., recognizing the importance of 'original documents,' are endeavoring to secure contemporary copies of early travels, voyages, and historical accounts, from which all historical deductions must be drawn. Americana has become scarce and is destined to become more so."

In 1920 the Arthur H. Clark Company catalog again emphasized that "by far the larger part of the copies (of original documents and rare books) now available are finding their way permanently into the libraries of public institutions from whence they will never again come upon the market."

This represented the climate at the time Fred entered the book business, obviously a difficult enterprise under these circumstances, but a more rewarding one for the ingenious dealer who could acquire items of scarce Americana. In fact, during the time he was operating the Denver Book Shop, Fred worked closely with the Denver Public Library. Chalmers Hadley, then city librarian, urged him to phone when he had obtained a new selection of books purchased from some private collection. "I want to be the first to look them over," he told Fred in those early days. "Sometimes when he came the books would still be piled on the floor, and Hadley wouldn't hesitate to get down on his hands and knees, in his fashionable suit, and go through them."

The personable proprietor of the Denver Book Shop made many friends who proved to be not only important confidants and sources for leads to collections, but also to provide him with expertise in the rare book field. One such person who was of particular help in the area of Western Americana was Lester Gehman, a retired major from the U.S. Army, who had started collecting books relating to the West early in the 1900s. He was exceptionally knowledgeable in the history and personalities of the West and willingly shared his storehouse with Fred.

Another valuable contact was his friend from his days with the Curran Company, Tracy Reeve, who introduced him to his father's fine collection of Americana that had its beginnings in the 1880s, before the elder Mr. Reeve left Princeton, Illinois, to make his home in Colorado. The subject matter of this library was American history generally, not confined to the West. After many visits, extensive browsing, and liberal borrowing privileges, Fred had acquired a broad familiarity with general Americana that would provide him with the background so essential to the particular interests that he eventually developed.

The Denver Book Shop had on its shelves hundreds of excellent volumes and a young proprietor who had accumulated an amazing amount of knowledge about book collecting in a relatively short time. It appeared, in the early months, that all of the ingredients for success were there. But, partly due to the poor location, the lack of capital, and perhaps a bit of inexperience (for years Fred had been ingenious in buying books, but had done little selling of books), the store did not prosper and by the end of 1922 the outlook was discouraging.

The year 1923 would be a golden year for American literature, with such classics being published as Sinclair Lewis's *Babbitt,* T. S. Eliot's *The Waste Land,* and Robert Frost's second volume of verse, *North of Boston*. It was the heyday for writers: Joseph Conrad, Carl Sandburg, Vachel Lindsay, Willa Cather, F. Scott Fitzgerald, John Dos Passos, Aldous Huxley, Somerset Maugham, and on and on.

But for Fred Rosenstock it was the year he closed the Denver Book Shop. Early in 1923 he made the decision, starting to sell his stock down and to remove some of the better books to his home. He probably could have liquidated his inventory by selling the entire collection to another dealer at a substantial discount, but Fred, with an innovative flair, prepared to stage Denver's first book auction in June of 1923.

He hired a young auctioneer, agreeing to give him twenty percent of the proceeds, then sent out about five hundred postcards advertising the event. A goodly crowd was there and Fred was confident that the sale would go well. The auctioneer rapped his gavel and offered a beautiful multi-volume set of Charles Dickens. The bidding was slow and low. Fred watched with disappointment, finally realizing that the auctioneer knew the auction business, but not books. After the first few sets had been sold at a suicidal sacrifice, Fred called the auctioneer aside for a strategy meeting. They decided that before each bidding, Fred himself would describe the merchandise: the author, the edition, binding, condition, significance. This was the magic touch. From then on activity increased and most of the sets and bindings brought realistic prices.

After the public auction, there were still several thousand individual, miscellaneous books left on the shelves, and four or five of Fred's bookseller friends were standing around, a bit unhappy since it had been rather slim pickings for them to that point. Fred suggested that they could select any books they wanted, place them in stacks, and he would make them a lot price, an offer they were pleased to accept. When he finally closed the door of the Denver Book Shop for the last time, all the merchandise of any value had been sold. The young Rosenstock concluded that, in the face of adversity, it had been a successful auction.

A lesser man may have been disheartened by the failure of his first venture, resolving to seek other avenues that might prove more lucrative. Actually, Fred's experience convinced him that he liked the business and, after a careful analysis, concluded that most of his mistakes were the result of a lack of know-how. "I didn't say, *if* there's a next time — I said to myself, 'The next time will be different,' for I was already planning for that while that young auctioneer was selling my stock."

Fortunately Fred had many other talents — as a bookkeeper, stenographer, salesman. He had also acquired patience. It would be several years before Denver would see another Fred Rosenstock bookstore, but in the interim he continued to read, to keep up his contacts with his dealer friends, and he went on buying books. "I gradually learned to tell the difference between the more and less valuable books and picked up more and more information about first editions and Americana. Now and then I was able to find a real bargain in dealer catalogs."

Even before the Denver Book Shop had closed in the summer of 1923, Fred had met an aggressive real estate man by the name of Joseph DeRose. They formed a friendship which would blossom into a business relationship that not only would last for many years, but would provide Fred with a diversification of experience that would be of significance to his ultimate success in the world of business.

Fred Rosenstock's initial experience as a bookseller, despite the adversities and ultimate failure, proved to be an important training period, enabling him to acquire a background and friendships that would serve him well in his newly adopted Colorado home. He had made his mark as a book dealer and collector, and had achieved acceptance by his Denver peers.

CHAPTER III

A HARD FREEDOM

ONLY TWO DECADES before the failure of the Denver Book Shop Fred Rosenstock had arrived in America, a nine-year-old Jewish immigrant boy from Austria-Hungary. The moment of the docking of the good ship *Patrizia* was memorable.

Those hundreds of immigrants crowding along the rail on the upper deck — Jews, Russians, Czechs, Poles, Hungarians — could only see the New York skyline, the sleek, tall buildings of Manhattan, the graceful church spires, and the dozens of piers jutting out into the harbor. They could not see the tenements, the squalor of the minority neighborhoods, the heat and stench of the sweatshops where many of these newcomers would soon be employed, working six days a week from pre-dawn to darkness.

For some, like the Rosenstocks and the Ashenbergs, this was a time for reuniting the family once again (Abraham had emigrated two years earlier), for others it was a hoped-for opportunity in a new land, and for still others it was an escape from persecution and near-slavery to a future that could only be an improvement. To Fred, whose mother had scrubbed him clean and dressed him in a clean shirt and his best short pants, it was a moment of great excitement: he would soon be seeing his father again.

The reunion was delayed for two days at Ellis Island, the immigration station that had replaced picturesque Castle Gardens, which had been the landing place for immigrants until 1891. These were anxious hours for Leah and restless ones for Fred and sister Anne, but finally the wait was over and Abraham, accompanied by Uncle Morris Ashenberg, embraced the family, amid hugs and tears. Abraham, despite his meagre resources, had purchased a new suit with short trousers and long black stockings for his son, a frilly dress for Anne, and a gaily colored scarf for Leah.

Never had Fred seen such a great city — over 4.5 million people lived on this fabulous island of Manhattan, and already dozens of skyscrapers towered above the streets. Built in the 1890s were the twenty-six-story World Building, and the twenty-story "Flatiron" Building, flanked by numerous other structures from ten to fifteen stories, a phenomenal sky-line for the first days of the twentieth century. Unfortunately, the time for sightseeing was limited, and the Ashenberg-Rosenstock entourage moved quickly in a carriage to the Grand Central Station, there to board the New York Central for Rochester, over 300 miles away.

The train trip started north, up the Hudson, high bluffs on the one side and the river on the other. It was late summer of 1904, and the hills were wearing their finest greenery, and the trees along the Hudson — elm, maple, cottonwoods — were in full foliage. Night had fallen before the train reached the state capital of Albany, and it was still dark when the Rosenstocks reached the burgeoning city of Rochester.

For a brief time — perhaps two weeks — the Rosenstocks lived with Fred's Uncle Meyer, while Leah searched for a place that would be adequate, and still affordable, on a salary of eight to ten dollars a week. Fred quickly made friends with a boy his age, Clayton Schnarr, who lived next door. Clayton spoke only English, and Fred knew German, Ruthenian, and Yiddish. But language proved no barrier and in the short period he lived there they found a variety of common interests, the most exciting of which, to Fred, was baseball. It was a sport sweeping America, a part of an increase in spectator sports in general. The National League had been formed in 1876, but the American League was less than ten years old when the Rosenstocks arrived in Rochester. Sand-lot baseball and semi-professional leagues existed in small towns every-where, and early in the twentieth century cities such as Rochester,

Buffalo, Albany, and Toronto had been granted franchises for minor league play.

Rochester, located on Lake Ontario at the mouth of the Genesee River, was a sprawling, expanding city of 175,000 in 1904. Originally the region was the home of the Seneca Indians, but by 1811, when Colonel Nathaniel Rochester offered the first lots for sale, the Senecas, along with the rest of the Iroquois, had been pushed westward or confined to reservations. Known as Rochesterville initially, it was one of a cluster of villages along the Genesee until the opening of the Erie Canal in 1823, when Rochester absorbed the other communities. Strategically positioned in the heart of a rich agricultural area, with wheat one of the principal products, the city utilized cheap water power from the Genesee and the Erie Canal transportation system to parlay its future to one of a leading milling center in this young country. But with the increased tempo of westward migration during the twentieth century the Midwest replaced the East as the country's breadbasket, and Rochester lost its title of "The Flour City," replacing it with "The Flower City" as it became a primary center for nurseries, with more than thirty nurseries flourishing by 1900.

Of greater significance to the Rosenstocks — and the Jewish immigrants in general — was Rochester's shoe and clothing industry, a part of the town's economy from its earliest days, gaining momentum after the Civil War with the invention of new machinery, the industrial revolution, and the coming of hordes of immigrants skilled in the needle trades. The earliest arrivals, mostly German Jews, became the entrepreneurs and largely the owners and managers of the garment manufacturing companies. Ultimately, the east European Jews became the workers and the German Jews the bosses. Abraham Rosenstock, with his limited and meager finances, represented, comparatively, the more affluent of the Jewish immigrants coming at that time. According to a government report, the average Jewish immigrant in 1900 arrived at Ellis Island with an average of $15.00, and no marketable skills nor a knowledge of the language.

At the turn of the century, thirty-four percent of the Jews in America were employed in the clothing industry. If they were not already skilled, sewing was an occupation they could learn quickly; with most of the industry controlled by Jews, it was perhaps easier for them to obtain employment, and, finally, most of the clothing industry was located on the East Coast, close to their point of debarkation, a factor quite important when most had no money for further travel.

Rufus Learsi, in his book, *The Jews in America,* described the plight of the average Jewish immigrant: "They fled from persecution and found refuge in the land of liberty and opportunity, but for several decades of the mass influx, opportunity for the great majority of them was only a dream, and liberty meant freedom to toil like galley slaves or starve. In the mid-twentieth century the economic status of the Jews in America was one of dignity and competence, but most of them were perhaps unaware of the bitter struggle for subsistence which the immigrants of those early decades had to wage, and in their modern apartments in the cities and suburbs of the land, they rarely thought of the squalid tenements in the 'ghettos' of the big cities to which their forebears were condemned."

Compared to their small but adequate farm home in Biala Potok, the Rosenstocks' first "home" in America was hardly the dream house that many who came to this land of opportunity anticipated. The address was 98½ Joseph Avenue, in a commercial district, convenient to Abraham's clothing factory, but a location with few aesthetic advantages. A three-room flat, above a clothing store, reached by climbing nearly thirty steep steps, then fumbling one's way along a dark hallway to the rear (the "front" flat was occupied by the owner of the clothing store), walking down three steps and opening the door to the kitchen. The kitchen was hardly appealing: narrow, pullman-style, with tired wooden cupboards, a cast-iron sink and a small, coal-burning stove. The core of the flat consisted of a living-dining room area, which also served as a bedroom for Abraham, Leah and daughter Anne. An alcove off the living room was converted into a bedroom for Uncle Morris, who lined the walls with over three hundred volumes of books. At one end of the living room was an oversize closet, and a cot was installed in this "choice" location for Fred.

Although he had attended the equivalent of the fourth grade in Biala Potok and Czernowitz in Austria, he was required to start over in the first grade in Rochester, primarily since he had virtually no knowledge of English. However, he had a sound basis in language — being able to speak three languages and understand four. His teachers recognized his abilities and quickly advanced him to grades with children his own age.

"I suppose the incident of my reading so avidly of Napoleon's life in English while I was still in Austria," Fred recalled, "and the German-English dictionary that my Uncle Morris gave me along with other books in English, provided me with a pre-knowledge of the language. I don't recall any of the other students making fun of me, though they did refer to me as a 'greenhorn,' which was the term used for foreigners.

"I caught on to the English language very quickly, and I really don't remember speaking with an accent. Not just in recent times, but even fifty years ago when I would tell people I'd been born in Europe they'd be surprised. 'You have no accent,' they would say. I don't remember *ever* having a foreign accent."

An exceptional student, Fred received grades above normal. The Jewish community in Rochester was sizeable, and before too long Fred was attending a Hebrew school, superficially offering the same doctrines as in Austria, but without the emotional overtones that existed in eastern Europe, partially since Jews in the old country were bound together as a means of survival, a circumstance true in America to a much lesser degree. "Again I was put into a class with older kids. In those days, the system wasn't by grades. There were eight-year-olds, twelve-year-olds, and even thirteen-year-olds who were ready for their confirmation. They would all be put together, and even if you were eight — I was about nine at the time — you had to learn in unison with all the others.

It was easy for me, and I had no trouble catching up with the others in the class.

"But even at that early age, for some reason, the reading of the Bible made me skeptical. I don't mean I doubted the existence of God, or His ultimate wisdom. I was concerned with what man did *in the name of God*. I was then, and still am, upset with the repetition all through the Bible — here again, the way it was written was man's work. But things like people venerating to the Highest, and saying over and over again: 'Thou art the Highest, Thou hast the great power. We are like sand, a grain of sand on the shore compared to You. You have the power to do anything with us. We rely on You. We venerate You.' And this keeps reappearing, over and over again. I would think to myself, 'Why do they have to say it so many times? Why can't they do away with this adulation and so on in a few words? Isn't it enough to say it once? Certainly I wasn't criticizing God, but maybe, as literature, I think the Bible could have been written better.

"I decided that this wasn't the word of God — at least, not literally — but rather man-made statements. I couldn't be convinced that these came direct from Above. I was impressed with some of the interesting stories — like the flood and the crossing of the Red Sea, the escape from Egypt, and the fact that the Jews were slaves. That was history.

"I liked the ritual, the music, some of the celebratory things. Even in later years I enjoyed the special hymns and the way they were sung. I guess you might say I enjoyed the beautiful part of religion, and the art that was part of it."

To a nine- or ten-year-old, living in a new land with new friends and new games to play, school and Bible studies were a deterrent to a far more interesting way of life. In Fred's words, "There was always something doing on the outside. Kids didn't have the choice of so many things to do in Czernowitz. In Rochester there was always a baseball game. Even while you were studying the Bible, you were thinking about whether you were going to do the pitching or play first base.

"In Europe the Jewish kids were more confined. The synagogue and the Bible school loomed as a far more important thing in your life than in this country. The cold fact was that to me (at that young age) — and to most of the Jewish kids — baseball was a lot more fun than religion."

And young Fred Rosenstock had become a baseball addict. Not only did he enjoy the game as a participant, but he followed the major league players avidly, knowing by heart the batting averages of the sluggers, the won and the lost records of the pitchers, and the team standings in both the National and American Leagues. It was this enthusiasm that led to the closest scrape he ever had with the law. One afternoon the usual gang assembled to play a game when it was discovered they had no baseball. The young minds analyzed the problem and elected three of their players to acquire a baseball surreptiously from the neighborhood novelty store. Fred Rosenstock was one of the three. The first boy would be the lookout while the other two would wait for his signal and then make the heist. Fred and his companion walked into the store, extremely nervous and trying quite unsuccessfully to be casual as they walked up and down the counters before reaching the baseball display. The lookout indicated that all was clear, and Fred grasped the baseball in his sweaty palm. At that moment the heavy hand of the store manager gripped his shoulder.

The manager decided to mete out his own form of punishment in lieu of calling the police. He took the would-be thieves to the basement and tied them to a post, leaving them for three hours in total darkness. Such self-styled justice would be frowned on today, but it was effective. Fred was in a state of near panic during his confinement, vowing over and over that never again would he take anything that didn't belong to him.

His love of sports was not deterred, however, and he eventually became a fair tennis player, and an enthusiastic football and boxing fan as an adult. When he later developed his extensive rare book collection his primary field was Western Americana, but he accumulated an extensive library of books on sports that were never offered for sale.

In the fall of 1904, only a few weeks after his arrival, young Fred

Rosenstock was exposed to his first Presidential campaign. Colorful Teddy Roosevelt as the incumbent was running against placid, drab Judge Alton B. Parker of New York. While the outcome of the race was never in doubt — Roosevelt won every state outside of the Solid South — the banners, campaign buttons, the speeches, the torch parades, and the heated arguments he heard at every street corner were all part of a fascinating, novel excitement.

The early years were difficult for the Rosenstocks. Abraham, who disliked working in the garment industry and deplored the poor wages and working conditions, earned but little when employed, and frequently — making life even more desperate — he was not working at all. Actively supporting the union movements which were rampant at the time, Abraham was not endeared to his employers and often was the first to go, his employers advising him that rabblerousers were not welcome. During such periods, the few dollars a week Fred earned selling newspapers kept food on the Rosenstock table.

They were not alone in their hardship. The influx of immigrants kept increasing, from 300,000 annually during the 1870s, to 500,000 in the eighties and approaching 900,000 in the first decade of the new century. By the 1890s there was a growing resentment toward the immigrants who were held responsible for most of the country's ills, from depressed wages to causing the conditions that led to disease, vice, and crime associated with urban slums.

While ghettoes did not exist as such in Rochester, there were ethnic sections and neighborhoods — Jewish, Polish, Russian, Slavic. Except for the Jews, who lived closer to the heart of the city, many of the other minorities lived on the fringes, bought or rented a small piece of ground and developed small farms in the fertile Genesee Valley, growing fruits and vegetables and raising chickens and a few cows, continuing to live much as they had in Europe.

"We lived in a Jewish section, an area that included fifteen or twenty streets," Fred recalled, "and the population was at least fifty percent Jewish. The Jews were pretty much congregated there — these were not the wealthy German Jews, but those who came later from eastern Europe.

"We used to speak of 'Polack' Town. We didn't use the word 'Poles' or Polish. They were Polacks. There was also an Italian section, and each section, even the Jewish, had its share of organized gangs. And there'd be battles — usually planned in advance, almost like a military maneuver — with perhaps fifty or sixty Polish kids invading the Jewish section. We knew they were coming and would be ready for them. There would be a lot of fist fighting, throwing stones, using clubs, but never any guns, any shooting.

"I was too little to participate in anything like that. But even then things were fearful, and a Jewish kid wouldn't venture out of his area unless he had very real, important business. The Polish weren't too bad — you might get punched or knocked down. But the Italian kids — you had to be afraid of them because they were knife wielders. Maybe they weren't really, but that was the reputation they had in our neighborhood. There were very few Negroes in Rochester. I had a Negro friend when I went to school, named Chester. A pretty good ball player. But he was the only Negro in a class of about forty-five."

If there was occasional violence on the streets, it was sometimes matched in the small flat at 98½ Joseph Avenue. Fred had, almost from the time he could talk, a musical talent and an excellent singing voice. Whether his parents made a barter arrangement with a music teacher, or actually paid for lessons out of their meager earnings, the fact was that Fred started taking violin lessons. But baseball was more important and much more fun to practice than the violin. In the evening, when Abraham had returned from his job, fingers bleeding from the needles and his body tired from the long hours, Fred's mother would recount the day's activities, particularly stressing Fred's refusal to practice. Abraham's eyes would become cold as they focused on his son, and Fred would start to run, his father in pursuit. Finally the young boy would seek refuge under the large dining room table, but it was only a temporary haven. Eventually he was dragged out to receive the inevitable beating. "And then," Fred recounted, "my mother would come to my defense, urging my father to go easy on me." Ultimately, baseball was declared the winner and Fred's formal musical training came to an end.

There was always music in the house, even after the violin had disappeared. Fred's father, between fits of temper, had a likeable disposition and often had friends over in the evening. Fred would be sent to the neighborhood tavern to get a pitcher of beer and would then retire to his cot in the closet and listen to his father sing Yiddish and Hebrew songs in his strong, clear voice.

The Rosenstocks lived in the flat until 1910, moving to 19 Leopold Street shortly after Fred had graduated from the No. 9 Elementary School. Primarily Jewish in character, the neighborhood was residential, and the second story apartment was part of a house, with separate bedrooms for the children. Fred was enrolled in East High School that fall, but by the end of his sophomore year the family's financial problems had become critical and, following a series of conferences between the Rosenstocks and his Ashenberg uncles, he was withdrawn and arrangements made for him to attend the Rochester Business Institute. This was a difficult decision for Abraham who was basically a scholar and naturally had high hopes for his only son. But he was forced to agree that practical training in bookkeeping, shorthand and other office skills would produce the vitally needed income much sooner than if Fred were to complete high school.

Obviously Abraham was faced with other difficult decisions. While the need for money was great, he continued to be an activist in union activities. And the unions were growing. The Amalgamated Clothing Workers of America was launched in 1900, along with the International Ladies Garment Workers Union — two unions that were to remain among the strongest in the United States. In 1910 bitterness and violence marked "The Great Revolt," a strike of 60,000 cloak makers in New York City that was supported by numerous local strikes in other garment centers, including Rochester.

Fred found business school to his liking, and completed the year's course in seven months. At the urging of the school's director, and with his two uncles agreeing to underwrite additional courses in shorthand and typing, Fred continued on for a few months. So fast and accurate was his shorthand that his instructors used him to give exhibitions to the other students.

The year was 1913 and Fred had reached his eighteenth year when he obtained his first job. He was enthusiastic about the opportunity to earn his own money, and to help support his family, and took the first position offered — a bookkeeper-stenographer with the Willsea Works, one of several iron foundries in Rochester. He had no office to screen out the constant racket of the foundry, which not only made it difficult to concentrate, but soon got on his nerves.

With the impetuousness of youth, Fred decided to leave, convinced that he could find some position more to his liking. So one morning, after hardly a week's employment, he didn't show up for work. Several days later, when Abraham learned of his son's inexcusable method of resigning, he insisted that Fred face his employer in person and apologize for his actions. Difficult as it was, the young man realized that he had made a serious mistake in judgment, and went back to the Willsea Works and expressed his regrets at his actions, eating humble pie.

Being personable and having achieved such exceptional shorthand and typing prowess, he had no difficulty in finding another job. He was more selective, deciding to work for the Thomas Cusack Outdoor Advertising Company, again as a bookkeeper-stenographer. The automobile was becoming a way of life and with the building of serviceable roads the outdoor advertising business was booming. At Cusack, Fred's boss was a fiery, red-headed Irishman whose vocabulary was frequently punctuated with graphic, four-letter, Anglo-Saxon words. The young, inexperienced Rosenstock was shaken by the vigorous mannerisms and strong language, but eventually Fred became accustomed to the big Irishman and they became good friends. So pleased was the company with his work that he was offered a substantial promotion in the regional offices in Buffalo, some seventy-five miles away.

He turned down the opportunity, having received an offer to become the assistant secretary of the Rochester Chamber of Commerce. It was here that he demonstrated his abilities to organize and operate a business, and in a few months he was appointed office manager, directing a large staff, supervising the publication of a Chamber of Commerce magazine, selling advertising, and still handling a substantial amount of secretarial work. Although he had qualified assistants, Fred continued to record the minutes of important meetings in shorthand.

Rochester was a city with much to offer — not only to industry, but to tourists and residents as well. Three beautiful falls along the Genesee cascaded within the city limits, and thousands of acres of virgin land were reserved for parks — the Rochester Park Commission, one of the first, was established in 1888. The climate and soil were ideal for flowers, shrubs, and trees, one of the reasons why the city became a nursery center. Highland Park, with more than a hundred acres, is even today especially noted for its botanical gardens, and visitors from hundreds of miles attend the special flower show held at Easter, and still more throng there in May or June to enjoy the masses of lilacs in endless varieties.

And at the northern edge of the city was Lake Ontario, dotted with numerous sandy beaches and state parks. On many a Sunday afternoon the Rosenstocks would pack up a lunch, board one of the stubby little trolley cars and head for the beach. At the Lake Ontario horizon line, the long, low-slung freighters could be seen moving lazily en route to Buffalo or Toronto.

Another of Fred's interests in his early years in Rochester was the theatre. Unfortunately, during the first decades of the twentieth century serious plays of the legitimate theatre were being overshadowed by melodrama, vaudeville, and burlesque shows. Rochester, along with other eastern cities, had its share of popular playhouses and admissions for ten or twenty cents. At every opportunity, young Fred Rosenstock would sneak off to the theatre, getting the cheapest tickets possible, usually far in the last balcony, where he might watch such dramas as *Only a Working Girl,* or *Under the Gaslight*. Westerns were much in vogue, thanks in large measure to the exploits of Buffalo Bill and his Wild West Show. Some of the more popular titles were *The Scouts of the Plains, The Gambler of the West,* and *The First Scalp for Custer.*

With Fred making a substantial contribution to the family income, the worst of the economic crisis was over for the Rosenstocks, and in 1915 they moved into a home at 31 Leopold Street, the first house they lived in since they left their cottage in Biala Potok.

It appeared that young Fred Rosenstock, at twenty-two, was becoming established in the business community of Rochester. His responsibilities, after two years with the Chamber of Commerce, were greater, his enthusiasm increasing, his love of books developing into a more significant hobby. But on May 18, 1917, Congress passed the Selective Service Act requiring all men between the ages of twenty-one and thirty to register for military service.

Europe had already been at war since Archduke Francis Ferdinand was assassinated in 1914, and despite Woodrow Wilson's assurances that he would keep America out of the conflict, the battle clouds were becoming ominous and ever closer.

Soon this young Jewish immigrant would leave his post at the Chamber of Commerce, joining with millions of other young Americans to do his part in this war to end all wars.

CHAPTER IV

LOVE & WAR

THE ROSENSTOCKS, like most Americans, were shocked in the early days of August, 1914, when Germany declared war on Russia, the prelude to World War I, but it was the hope of the great majority — and perhaps the hope of the immigrants from eastern Europe even more so — that the United States would not become involved. When President Woodrow Wilson issued the first of his series of Proclamations of Neutrality on August 4, the populace cheered, wanting to be convinced that the conflict would remain an Old World conflagration.

By 1917, however, American neutrality existed only as a paper tribute, and few Americans were surprised when President Wilson in his inaugural address on March 5, 1917, indirectly suggested that war was inevitable. Less than a month later the President advised Congress to declare war, and the official declaration came on April 6 with a joint resolution to the effect that "the state of war between the United States and the Imperial German government which has thus been thrust upon the United States is hereby formally declared."

On December 7, 1917, when a formal act of war was passed against Austria-Hungary, it was an emotional moment for Fred Rosenstock and his family. But there was no waivering of their allegiance to their new homeland. Especially in the latter days, life in Austria-Hungary had been uneasy and whatever nationalism may have existed had been obliterated long before they came to America. In Fred's words: "My father became a citizen in 1910 and there was never any doubt as to where our loyalties lay. This was our country and we loved it."

It was a time of fervent patriotism, a nation united in its determination to, in President Wilson's idealistic words, "make the world safe for democracy." The few dissident intellectuals or pro-German sympathizers who dared speak out were silenced, jailed or otherwise suppressed. The pens of the cartoonists and the editorial writers spewed out propaganda designed to heighten American emotionalism, depicting the Germans as dark, evil-eyed Huns from the Asian steppes out to destroy the civilization and freedoms of the West.

Young Fred Rosenstock was secure in his position at the Rochester Chamber of Commerce, highly regarded, well-paid, with constantly increasing responsibilities and more promotions in the offing. Being nearsighted and having worn strong glasses from the time he was a child, and contributing substantially to his family's welfare, it was doubtful that he would have been drafted, and less likely that he would ever see combat. But the patriotic excitement was present in every young man's breast, including Fred's, and he became impatient to serve his country.

At Fred's request, Roland B. Woodward, the secretary of the Chamber of Commerce, wrote a letter of recommendation to an acquaintance of his in the War Department, and shortly thereafter Fred went to Washington for an interview. There was an acute shortage of young men, particularly with expert shorthand and typing skills, and Fred scored high in the tests and was immediately hired as a civilian employee in the Surgeon General's office of the Medical Department. "My life changed in a hurry. They gave me two weeks in Rochester to straighten out my affairs."

In June, 1917, Fred boarded the Penn Central for Washington, confident and enthusiastic, impatient for the train to leave, paying little heed to his mother's tearful farewells and kindly admonitions to be careful and to take good care of himself.

Washington, more than any other city in the United States, was dramatically changed by the declaration of war. Government agencies and departments already in existence were greatly expanded and hundreds of new boards and bureaus were set up. The city took on an international flavor as the Allied Powers sent special war representatives (complete with elaborate entourages) to the nation's capital, and Pennsylvania Avenue was soon crowded with young men in a variety of uniforms: the Scots with plaid skirts and bare knees, the blue gray of the distinguished French officers, the smart appearance of the Italians in their olive garb.

Everything was in short supply. Private housing was virtually nonexistent, and hotels and boarding houses were shockingly overcrowded. Temporary shelters for women war workers were erected on the Union Station and Capitol plazas, and a massive construction program was undertaken to erect impermanent structures in the park between the Pan-American building and the Lincoln Memorial, and on many squares in the Mall around Sixth and B streets.

"At that time, the Army had commandeered a three-story house in the 2600 block of Pennsylvania Avenue for the Medical Department," Fred recalls, "that was typical of the old mansions except for the uniformed guards standing out front. The entry was a broad, long waiting room, and I had to walk up a wide, carpeted staircase — three flights. I went into this big office on the top floor and there was this distinguished, white-haired gentleman, William C. Gorgas, the Surgeon-General of the United States Army. It was quite a thrill." General Gorgas, a surgeon in the American Army in 1880, had received national recognition in his fight against yellow fever while stationed in Havana, Cuba, and later as chief sanitary officer of the Panama Canal.

"Of course, I didn't work directly for General Gorgas. I was assigned the job of taking dictation from twelve officers. Because of my unusual speed at shorthand, I often covered meetings — at which a lot of technical material was discussed — with anywhere from ten to thirty persons participating."

Within a few months, the Medical Department had outgrown its quarters in the mansion and moved to one of the new, temporary structures erected in the vicinity of Seventh and B streets. As a civilian, Fred was earning $150 a month, more than many of the officers. But by the time the Medical Department had moved, young Rosenstock had been formally inducted into the Army as a private, and his salary dropped to thirty dollars a month. After a couple of weeks, he was promoted to corporal, then to sergeant, and finally, to sergeant first class.

For the first few days after his arrival in Washington Fred stayed at a hotel, close to the Medical Department building. Someone had suggested he might get acquainted with other Jewish boys by visiting the YMHA (the Young Men's Hebrew Association). He took this advice, and one evening met Emil Yoelson, the younger half-brother of Al Jolson. Emil knew of a family with extra space not far from the Yoelson's house, and insisted that Fred take a room there.

"The landlady's name was Mrs. Lests, and the house was in the southwest section — a Jewish district. What I remember most about the place was the street it was on — it was called Four-and-a-Half Street. There was one other boarder, Hyman Prives, who was in the Army and eventually went overseas in active combat," Fred recalled. He and Emil Yoelson became close friends, and the young Yoelson frequently arranged dates for Fred with Jewish girls. "It wasn't long until I was getting my own dates," Fred related, "and they weren't all Jewish.

"As a result of my acquaintance with Emil I was invited to the Yoelson's home and I met his father, his sister, his younger brothers and, of course, his half-brother, *the* Al Jolson, and Harry, the oldest. Al didn't live there, but he and Harry — they were both in show business — would come from New York from time to time. In those days Al was performing in musical comedies, working for the Shuberts. Even though the children still living at home were his stepbrothers and stepsisters, the family remained very close.

"It became a Friday night ritual for me to go to the Yoelsons. They had a real Friday night dinner — the beginning of the Sabbath — and insisted that I be there. One weekend Al brought Eddie Cantor with him and, at my age, I was pretty much overawed, sitting there eating dinner with Al Jolson and Eddie Cantor. Probably because of Al, the Yoelsons were a pretty popular family in Washington. Because of my ties with them, I became acquainted with a lot of people whom I might not otherwise have met.

"I'd led a rather confined life in Rochester — in my own little group. I had five or six friends, no girl friends, not much of a social life at all." When he and Emil began teaming up on double-dates, they often ended the evening at a dance hall. Fred had never danced in Rochester, but with the brash confidence of youth, he learned in Washington on the dance floor. "I stepped on a few toes at first, but it didn't take long until I was a pretty good dancer."

Fred had always been interested in the theatre, an interest which was heightened through his acquaintance with Al and Harry Jolson. "I became a kind of amateur entertainer. At first Emil and I used to write some dialogue to entertain the friends who'd show up at the Yoelson's on weekends, and later we'd put on vaudeville acts at every opportunity — singing, dancing, telling jokes. I'm no expert, but I think Emil had a better voice than Al."

Papa Yoelson never fully approved of his son's activities on the stage, nor did he understand how a mere comedian in black face could achieve success. In the words of Al's brother, Harry, in his book, *Mistah Jolson*, "He (Father Yoelson) regretted deeply that his loved boy, Asa, had not become a cantor, or had not at least gone into the clothing business." President Wilson, seeking relaxation from the strain of the problems of a world war, frequently attended the theatre, and Al Jolson was one of his favorite entertainers. The President honored the comedian by inviting him to lunch one day at the White House. When Papa Yoelson read of the event in the newspapers, he was pleased, but it did not lessen his lifelong hatred for the theatre.

After his induction into the Army, Fred continued to live with the Lests, but was required to attend early morning drill each day. And in the evenings, primarily to earn extra money, he obtained permission to do stenographic work for the War Trade Board. Here he met Billy Rose, also a male stenographer and secretary to Bernard Baruch, chairman of the War Industries Board. Rose later became famous as the pro-

Army Sergeant Fred Rosenstock, 1918

ducer of some of Broadway's greatest musical comedies, along the way marrying such celebrities as Fanny Brice and Eleanor Holm.

Fred's life in Washington was busy, not only with his work, but with his social activities as well. He joined the YMCA and the YMHA, primarily for the athletic activities. "I used to spend a lot of time working out, using the barbells and doing quite a bit of running. One morning, as a part of our Army company drill, we staged some races and other events. I can't recall the competition, but I won the 100- and 220-yard dashes."

Washington has always been a center for parties and entertainment, and there was no slowdown during the war. With many military personnel stationed in the Capital, eligible young men were plentiful, and thousands of civilian workers, both male and female, had thronged to the city to staff the wartime bureaucracy. "In just a few months, it seemed like I knew practically everybody in Washington, and something was always going on — a party, a picnic, a dance. In fact, when it came to arranging a party — like a hayride — I was always the one selected to get the group together," Fred recalled.

"My experience in Washington was tremendous, a new life in every respect because everything that happened to me there was different from what had ever happened to me before, and I enjoyed every bit of it. And one thing that broadened my outlook was the change in my circle of friends. The preponderance of my friends had always been Jewish, because I lived among a Jewish group. But where I worked in the Surgeon General's office there were very few Jews, and I made many good friendships there. And about half of the girls I went out with were not Jewish. As time went on, my personal friendships actually became more numerous on the non-Jewish side."

In a way, Fred Rosenstock was a dual personality. Gregarious, outgoing, always ready to join a party, he still kept his love for books. By the time he had left Rochester, he had accumulated two or three hundred volumes, most of them picked up in secondhand stores and the Salvation Army, primarily on the subjects of sports or history.

"In Washington," he noted, "I continued to add to my library. I suppose — even then — you could call me a collector because I bought enough books to deserve the designation. I always had books, and it was one of the delights of my life. I wasn't in any town very long before I would go to a bookstore. I didn't get to meet the owners — I spent my time looking for books rather than talking to the people who owned them. But eventually I did get to know a few of the more important dealers and became friends with them. I recall one bookseller who really impressed me. Frankly, most of the bookstore owners weren't very knowledgeable. But this man, Luther Cornwall, was a prominent bookseller. After I went to Denver, I used to make buying trips to Washington and I'd always see him first. With Luther Cornwall, I would say, I made a friendship which counted for something.

"In those days, I hadn't developed an interest in first editions. Frankly, I wasn't aware of first editions as such, or the value, the quality, or the collectors' interest in them. I was influenced by the books themselves. When I bought a book, I bought it to read, not just to add to my library. And I never dreamed that I would one day be in the book business."

The Rosenstocks, one would have to say, were opportunists in the better sense of the word. Fred had kept in close contact with his family in Rochester, and felt strongly that they should be reunited in Washington, not only to bring the family together, but to take advantage of the economic potential existing in the wartime capital city. In the few hours of spare time he had, Fred searched for a house that he could rent, adequate for his father and mother, sister Anne, and his young nephew, Joseph Feldstein, who had been taken in by the Rosenstocks when Leah's sister, Joseph's mother, had died.

By the end of December, 1917, Fred had found a suitable home at 1145 Eighth Street, in a residential area but close to the trolley line which ran down Seventh Street to the heart of Washington. In January, 1918, the family moved to Washington. Abraham obtained a job with a dying and cleaning establishment, Anne became a stenographer at the

Department of Agriculture, and little Joseph, aged seven, started selling newspapers. "Joseph was a scrappy little fellow," Fred recalled, "who would often come home with a blackened eye that he got while fighting to hold onto his corner."

Abraham was earning three to four times the wages he had made in the garment factory, and soon had sufficient capital to open his own dry-cleaning and repair shop. His establishment was located in northeast Washington, in the Negro section, and he became affectionately known to his black customers as Abe. His business flourished. "He was as happy as he had ever been in his life," Fred related. "He was an expert tailor and did all the repair work himself, but sent the cleaning out. It was quite a change for a man who considered himself a scholar, and yet I think he was satisfied with his life."

It was inevitable that Fred, participating as he was with the young people in the social whirl of Washington, would eventually become involved seriously with a girl. He had a number of casual relationships, but in September of 1918 he met Jeannette Stadler, a volunteer worker in the Medical Department. She had come to Washington from St. Louis with her cousin, Jeannette Lebermuth, from Malden, Missouri, along with hundreds of other young girls swept up in a wave of patriotism and also looking forward to the excitement of being where the action was.

She was a beautiful, fair-skinned brunette, with an infectious smile and warm, brown eyes. While at a dance party, Fred watched her on the floor for most of the evening, finally asking her to dance. Before the first number was over, he had asked her for a date, and in the next month he took her out four or five times. Her family was affluent and a significant part of the social set in St. Louis. By November 11, 1918, the day of the Armistice, Fred was seeing Jeannette every day, and missing her during the hours they were apart.

The Armistice had come without warning, a sudden though welcome shock to the entire nation. But it meant, also, that lives would be changed, and Fred's immediate concern was what would happen to his romance with Jeannette. She, along with most of the volunteer workers, received her notice almost immediately. In ten days she would be leaving. Suddenly the bottom had dropped out of Fred's world. Not until he realized that she was no longer going to be a part of his life did he fully understand how much she had meant to him. "When Jeannette told me she would be returning to St. Louis, it was such a matter-of-fact statement that I thought she'd just say goodbye and that would be the end of it. But when I revealed my feelings, her response was delightful and thrilling. We had just come back from a Friday night movie, and I had taken her to her apartment. I really thought that was the end, but suddenly I was in a great new world. Usually, I didn't stay, but this important evening we talked long into the night, discussing the possibilities of our lives, the future.

"Jeannette told me she wanted to live in St. Louis, and that she wanted me to come there. Her father, who was an executive with the Carleton Wholesale Dry Goods Company, had many contacts and would find me a job or an opportunity to enter some business of my own. I told her that I'd rather make my own opportunities, but that I'd think about it. We decided to spend the entire day together on the following Sunday, the last day I'd have a chance to see her before she left."

The end of the war was a traumatic experience for Fred Rosenstock, as it was an emotional experience for the entire nation. In Washington, the celebration was spontaneous, starting within minutes after the announcement of the Armistice. "World War I, when that ended," Fred recalled, "total strangers were hugging and kissing each other. There were truckloads of people, almost in caravan, driving down the streets, some jumping off and others jumping on. Everybody was waving flags, blowing horns. I don't know where they got all the things so quickly. It went on for days, and everyone seemed to want to express the happiness they felt. There were signs praising President Wilson, even though he hadn't always been popular. Actually, most Americans had a great veneration for Woodrow Wilson. I remember being on the street when his limousine went by — and he'd be sitting there straight and tall with his stovepipe hat on — and people were proud of him." The nation, and the world, truly believed that this had been the war "to end all wars."

But by that Sunday, nearing the end of November, the celebrations were over and the city had achieved a degree of normalcy. It was early in the morning when Fred called for Jeannette and they started to walk toward the complex of government buildings, monuments, and the great Mall between the Capitol and the Lincoln Memorial. The young couple meandered through West Potomac Park, along the Tidal Basin, through the groves of Japanese cherry trees which provide a brilliant spectacle of pink and white when they bloom in early spring, but in late November were barren twigs against a sullen sky.

Before the day was over, they had climbed the slight hill to Washington Monument and were impressed as any tourist over the sight of the Capitol Dome, the White House, the buildings housing the Treasury Department, the United States Supreme Court, the State Department, a panorama of the seat of government of the greatest nation in the world.

"It was," Fred recollects nostalgically, "one of the most wonderful days of my life. People talk about walking on a cloud. That's how I felt about that Sunday. We agreed that after I got out of the service I'd get a job in Washington, save my money, and then come to St. Louis. At the time, it sounded like we had our lives planned, and that there would be nothing but sunshine and roses from then on."

With the end of World War I, in the words of H. L. Mencken, came the end of "an epoch of sweetness and light." A genteel middle-class culture had basically ruled American ideals and values for over a hundred years, strengthened by a national opinion united by the war. Woodrow Wilson epitomized this drive toward a singleness of purpose when he said, "Some day we shall be of one mind, our ideals fixed, our purposes harmonized, our nationality complete and consentaneous."

Writers and intellectuals like Mencken, Van Wyck Brooks, Randolph Bourne, and Ezra Pound rebelled against this genteel structure, stressing their disdain for the bourgeois values of the day. The American way of life, as well as the literary tastes, began to change. Sherwood Anderson's *Winesburg, Ohio,* and *The Education of Henry Adams,* portraying the desolation and despair of small town lives, became popular, along with Mencken's volume of essays, *Prejudices: First Series,* in which he mocked American materialism, enthusiasm, and cultural pretensions.

The necessity for increased productivity during the war gave rise, to a large extent through the War Industries Board, to standardization and simplification of thousands of products, which ultimately led to lower-priced goods in large quantities. When Henry Ford pioneered the assembly line and produced the Model T, the entire life-style of Americans was altered. With electric power extended to some eighty percent of the homes in the United States, appliances such as toasters, vacuum cleaners, refrigerators, coffee percolators, and radios added impetus to the change.

With surprising rapidity, the American structure was shifting from rural to urban. The farmers and the small town inhabitants were waging a desperate battle to retain the old culture, the old way of life.

And young men, such as Fred Rosenstock, waited impatiently for their release from military service so that they could challenge the new world. In Sergeant Rosenstock's case, four months were to pass before his discharge. It was a difficult period, now that the patriotic enthusiasm had dissipated and the work remaining was both minimal and dull. Fortunately during this period he was able to investigate various business opportunities, and when his papers came through on February 15, 1919, he was already virtually employed as a civilian.

The mid-Atlantic regional headquarters for the Thomas Cusack outdoor advertising company, the same organization Fred had worked for in Rochester, was located in Roslyn, Virginia, a suburb of Washington, and the company welcomed him back. "Primarily I was hired as a salesman, but I also spent a part of my time in the office, doing bookkeeping, handling correspondence and things like that." Business was booming, and young Rosenstock was aggressive, ambitious, and had the determination to make as much money as he could as fast as he could.

After all, Jeannette was waiting for him in St. Louis, and that fact was first and foremost in his mind.

He brought in several large contracts, and one day John Shoemaker, the district manager, called him into his office and asked if he'd like to take a trip to Minneapolis. "The Cusack Company had been trying for years to sell a contract to the Washburn-Crosby Company (which became Pillsbury, the Gold Medal Flour people). Signs along the railroads were the big thing then, and I was confident I could convince Washburn-Crosby of the value of a national billboard campaign along the railroad right-of-ways. Anyway, I accepted the assignment and came back with a contract for 200 signs. It was a big day, and a big commission."

In addition to selling for Cusack, Fred worked at the District National Bank in Washington at night checking passbooks and straightening out accounts. He had neither the time nor inclination to squander his earnings on social activities, content to watch his savings accumulate. By June of 1920 he had saved $5,000 and wrote to Jeannette that he was coming to St. Louis.

His intent was to resign from Cusack, but he decided to take a two week's vacation, in case his trip to St. Louis wasn't successful. "It had been almost two years since I'd seen Jeannette and even though we'd been corresponding I felt I shouldn't burn any bridges."

For well over a year he had been working night and day, and had become quite susceptible to colds, an affliction not uncommon in the damp Washington climate. He was thin and tired when he boarded the train for St. Louis, and looked forward not only to seeing Jeannette, but to some rest and relaxation.

When he stepped off the train, Jeannette was there, as beautiful as ever. But she hardly recognized him. "What's happened to you?" she asked. She scolded him mildly for not taking care of himself, and promised that she would cure him of his ills. En route to her home, they discussed their plans and decided that Fred would stay for two weeks and then they would announce their engagement.

The Stadlers were a sophisticated family, living in a large, rambling house designed for entertaining. Jeannette's parents were gracious, but Fred felt uncomfortable, the surroundings being so foreign to his relatively simple way of life.

On his first Sunday, Jeannette arranged for an outing at their private boat club, not so much to impress him as to give him an opportunity to meet some of her friends. Fred was not feeling well, and had never enjoyed being around water and had never learned to swim. At 5:30 that morning the young couple jumped on the electric trolley for the hour and a half journey to the club. Jeannette held his hand, excitedly assuring him that it would be a wonderful day and that everyone would love him.

It was only seven in the morning when they arrived, and within minutes Jeannette had changed into her swimsuit and was in the pool, urging Fred to join her. "I stood around for awhile, and finally felt the water. It was cold and the last thing I wanted to do was get in that pool. I looked at her friends, and every man there looked like Tarzan. Eventually I realized that I was 'losing out,' so I finally put on a swimsuit and jumped in the shallow end. Not being able to swim, I couldn't do much except splash around a little. I can't remember ever being so cold. I just stood there in the water, cold, shivering. I felt like I was the original 97-pound weakling."

By the time they left for home, Fred had a chill and was running a fever. The next day he began feeling worse, and by Tuesday Jeannette insisted that he see their family doctor. His temperature was 103.5, and the doctor urged him to go to the hospital. "I didn't want that — I wanted to get back to Washington. So Jeannette and her brother put me on the train. Everything had been left unresolved, and I was so sick at the time it didn't seem to matter."

The train ride was an eighteen-hour nightmare, as Fred's fever continued to worsen. When he arrived in Washington his family doctor immediately sent him to the hospital. It was no surprise when the doctor advised him that he had pneumonia. After three weeks in the hospital, Fred was released and advised to stay home and rest for another month.

But two weeks later he tried to go to work, had a relapse and went back to bed.

His condition stabilized, but he showed little improvement. "It's easy to get sick in Washington," Fred philosophized, "but you don't get well in Washington." His doctor concurred, advising him to relocate in a dry, desert climate like Arizona or California. "The Cusack people were wonderful. My boss, John Shoemaker, authorized the company to pay all of my expenses for the trip West, and offered to do whatever he could to help me find a new job."

Except for the brief visit to Minneapolis and his ill-fated trip to St. Louis, Fred had never been west of Cleveland. He wrote to Jeannette to inform her of the latest developments, and her response was immediate and reassuring. Facing an unknown future and with a deep concern over the state of his health, he felt he was being unfair in attempting to maintain a relationship with Jeannette, and felt it would only be fair to suggest a separation so that, in his words, "she could be free to live her own life without obligation to me."

And so, on a hot, humid day in August of 1920, a tired young man boarded a train once more, taking a westward journey that would be the most significant of his life. It was another beginning, and as the familiar sights of the Washington countryside faded, Fred Rosenstock removed his glasses, settled back in his seat and recalled his days as a child in Biala Potok while wondering what the future would bring.

CHAPTER V

THE VOYAGE OUT

FROM THE DOORSTEP the small boy could look across the potato field to the foothills of the Carpathian Mountains, the spectacular barrier between the Austrian province of Galicia and neighboring Rumania. It was springtime and the Mlynuuka River was full, and the boy could see his father, Abraham, standing by the side of the stream.

Selig Usher Rosenstock, too impatient to walk, ran the quarter mile to the river, reaching out for his father's hand when he arrived, breathless and with a grin on his face. It was an escape from feeding the geese and cleaning up after the chickens. And one of the few opportunities to meander along the Mlynuuka with his father at his side. They walked only a few yards when Abraham, smiling down, flopped on his back and picked up a few stones and started throwing them in the river. Selig watched the ripples, then joined in the game, trying to hit the center of the ripple.

It was late afternoon, and the tall man and his young son continued to throw stones until the sun started slipping behind the peaks of the Carpathians. "Selig," he said to the boy, looking away, "I'm going to America."

At the moment they were spoken, the words had no particular significance for Selig, for he was only six and "going to America" meant no more than "going to Belobozhnitsa," a town near Biala Potok, where Selig now lived and where he had been born in 1895. But the look on his father's face and the quiet way he spoke made the boy realize that playtime was over and that something important was about to happen.

[51]

During the next several days, Selig was aware of long and serious conversations between his father, his mother, and grandmother Ashenberg — and then his father was gone. "To America," his mother, Leah, told him, repeating the words softly. It would be two years before Selig would again see his father and the family would be reunited in the United States.

Selig's mother was an Ashenberg, a family which had lived for generations in Biala Potok, a community of two or three hundred, with less than half a dozen Jewish families. Most of the residents were Roman Catholic, and the Rosenstocks were tolerated but were in no way accepted as part of the social or political life. No outright persecution was inflicted upon them; rather they — as Jews — were subject to the punishment of isolation, heresy, and ridicule.

Life had become more tolerable for the Jewish people following the Compromise of 1867 which created the dual monarchy of Austria-Hungary and the subsequent coronation of Austria's Emperor Francis Joseph I as ruler of the newly formed country. With the adoption of a new constitution, Austria became a constitutional monarchy with far-reaching civil and individual liberties being provided to Austrian citizens. Of special significance to the Jews was the Article that gave all nationalities equal suffrage, with inalienable rights to each group to preserve its nationality and language. Unfortunately, these idealistic principles were feebly augmented, and living conditions for Jews throughout central and eastern Europe gradually deteriorated and more and more rights were denied them. Continuous outbreaks against the Jewish minority occurred, culminating in the riot of Prague in 1897.

Jewish leaders, foreseeing difficult times for their people in Europe, urged migration to other lands. One of the pioneers of national autonomy was Chayim Zhitlowsky, who rejected the idea of territorial concentration of Jews, pleading for mass migration from the countries of their origin. In the late nineteenth century, historian Simon M. Dubnow foresaw a mass transplantation of Jewry to America. Between 1880 and 1910 a substantial segment of the world's Jewish population — unable

Fred Rosenstock and sister Anne, Czernowitz, 1902

or unwilling to remain in Europe where economic opportunity was re-stricted and the hostile pressures increasing — was in a feverish migra-tory flight. As Yiddish centers in the United States were flourishing, the European centers were disappearing. New York City by 1905 had be-come the third greatest area of Jewish concentration, together with the traditional old world cities of Odessa and Warsaw.

Such were the underlying currents that ultimately forced the Rosen-stocks, the Ashenbergs and thousands of other Jewish families to forsake a land they had lived in for centuries to seek freedom and equality in the New World.

Abraham, a quiet and unassuming man, under normal circum-stances would have preferred to remain on his small farm in Biala Potok. Even with the deterioration of conditions, Selig's father would not have taken such a giant step without prodding. In the mid-1890s Morris and Meyer Ashenberg, Abraham's brothers-in-law, had joined the stream of emigrants crossing the Atlantic to America, found employment as tai-lors, and began to urge the rest of their families to come to the land of opportunity.

Abraham Rosenstock did not have the happiest of childhoods. Born of his father's second wife, he had no real family, only two older half-brothers, one a doctor and the other a merchant, and neither having any particular affection for their younger half-brother. When their father died Abraham — a boy of fifteen at the time — had to make his own way. The literacy rate in Galicia was one of the lowest in Austria; by 1910 it was only 54.1 percent, as compared to 81.3 percent for the coun-try as a whole. Abraham was gifted with a good mind, and found em-ployment during his difficult youthful years as a tutor to the children of wealthy parents in Budzanov, where he lived, and the neighboring towns of Belobozhnitsa and Chortkov. This was an unusual feat for there were few Jewish teachers, most Christians refusing to allow their children to learn from Jews.

Even such a non-hazardous occupation as tutoring had its tremulous moments. As recalled in later years, Anne Rosenstock Chesler — Selig's sister — related this incident. "While my father was teaching a student, the son of wealthy parents, the pupil was showing off a gun his father had just purchased and accidentally pulled the trigger, wounding my father quite badly in the back. He was hospitalized for several weeks, with the boy's parents paying all the medical bills, offering also to pay for an operation to have the bullet removed from his back.

"Luckily it lodged in an area where — according to the doctor — it would not really be painful if he managed to maintain a certain weight. My father refused the operation and went through life — he lived to be ninety-one — with this bullet in his back."

Following his marriage to Rachel Leah Ashenberg, Abraham assisted with the chores at the farm home in Biala Potok and continued his tutoring. On special holidays he served as cantor in the synagogue at Belobozhnitsa.

It was 1902 when Abraham Rosenstock said his farewells to his wife and children and headed for America to join his brothers-in-law and accumulate the funds necessary to bring his family. Selig, nearing seven, became the man of the house, bringing in the wood, taking care of the chickens and geese, while his mother took in sewing, worked in the potato fields, and left the cooking to Grandmother Ashenberg.

Biala Potok, being a small, non-Jewish town, had no Hebrew school, and Selig attended an Austrian public school, learning both German and Ruthenian languages. He was a good student, having inherited a love of reading and good books from his father. When his Uncle Morris brought him a book on Napoleon from America, Selig became enamored of the little general's military exploits. "I wanted to tell the whole world about Napoleon," he reminisced, "and tried to re-create the battles I read about by drawing them on the side of our newly painted white house with black crayon."

After Abraham had left, the burden of caring for the farm became more difficult and the decision was made to move to Czernowitz, some seventy miles to the south, in the province of Bucovina, where they could live with Leah's sister, Ada. Legally and technically Jews were free to move at will, but in Biala Potok, where they formed such a small minority, there was a considerable amount of antagonism and anti-Semitism, and the Rosenstocks felt some concern for their safety as they prepared to leave.

In Selig's words: "The Jews, even in that day, showed a certain stability, a progressiveness, and this created jealousy among the so-called Christians. But in our particular case there was something more specific. It was a long-smouldering animosity between my grandmother and an old neighbor woman. This was a long-standing feud — maybe of forty or fifty years duration. She found out that we were planning to go to America, and this old antagonist of my grandmother was reported to have said that she wouldn't let her leave alive."

It was ironic that their unfriendly neighbor was adamant in her determination that they stay. But whether her threats were real or merely a way of life, the Rosenstocks decided to leave clandestinely. A driver and wagon were hired, and the time of departure was set for four A.M. "We had sold everything," Selig recalled, "except for some of our bedding and kitchen dishes. It was still sort of dark, and we drove along with a single horse and a little cart — my grandmother, my mother and I, and my little sister. The horse didn't go very fast, sort of ambled along, and this bothered me. All the talk prior to our departure had concerned me and I was perhaps more scared than the grownups. I kept looking back, and after daylight broke I began wondering if our neighbors had discovered we were gone and were following us. But soon we were into country I hadn't seen before and there were so many other things of interest that I lost the fear and forgot the old woman and her threats of violence." Actually the family traveled only a few miles by wagon, boarding a train at a nearby town for the journey south to Czernowitz.

Czernowitz was a large city, the capital of Bucovina Province and the seat of a large university built in 1875. Jews tended to congregate in the large population centers, and there was a substantial Jewish area in Czernowitz. Selig's Aunt Ada and her husband, Zigmund Kremnitz, had a large two-story house in the Hebrew section with a porch extending the full length of the front, facing the street. For that period it was extremely modern, with both running water and inside toilets.

"We lived in Czernowitz for a year," Selig recalled, "waiting to leave for America. My father wasn't ready to bring us, making eight to ten dollars a week as a tailor. He was actually a scholar, a student, and he never truly became successful in his menial trade. We were anxious to start our new life, but at the same time I enjoyed my stay in Czernowitz. There was a good Hebrew school, about a block from our house, run by a teacher who was sort of a semi-Rabbi. There were about thirty students in my class — and I was the youngest. I was sort of a "whiz kid," and almost overnight I found myself holding my own in a class with fourteen-year-olds.

"The Rabbi — that's what we called him, even though he really wasn't — was impressed with my voice, and he would have me sing certain religious verses. And that made me a special pupil."

Selig's love of books, which would play an important part in his later years, started with his stay in Czernowitz. "There were fine book stores, rows upon rows of wonderful books. We think of paperbacks as being a recent innovation, but some of the stores in Czernowitz had hundreds of paperbacks lining the shelves — mostly classics. My Uncle Morris perhaps had the greatest influence on me as far as my interest in books was concerned. When he returned to Czernowitz from America to arrange for our departure, he brought several books, written in English, for me to read. I didn't know English, only German, Ruthenian, and Polish conversationally, but not grammatically. He also brought me a little German-English dictionary. I was only seven or eight at the time, but I was soon able to read the books and understand what was in them. It was my Uncle Morris who would take me to the bookstores — and I was fascinated with them, even then."

On weekends and during the summer when school had recessed, Selig would sometimes ride with his Uncle Zigmund to the Czernowitz railroad station, one of the newer and more elaborate structures in the city at that time. His uncle drove a horse-drawn cab — today it would be the equivalent of a limousine — wearing a handsome uniform, standing tall and erect beside his ornate carriage as he waited for a fare.

In Biala Potok Selig had virtually no friends his own age, and most of the games he played were dependent upon his own imagination. But attending a Hebrew school in Czernowitz, he had many friends and learned such formalized games as hide-and-seek, capture the flag, and red light. The year or so he spent in Czernowitz were the golden days of his childhood and perhaps the most significant.

The province of Bucovina, like Galicia, was rolling foothill country and high mountains, a part of the Carpathian range. Anciently known as Turkish Moldavia, it was ceded to Austria in 1777 and in 1849 became a separate crown-land, an area of approximately 4,000 square miles. Despite the modern capital city of Czernowitz and its new university, the literacy rate for the entire province was less than fifty percent. Lumbering in the thickly forested Carpathians, and sheep and cattle-grazing on the lower slopes have been the primary occupations for centuries. With the advent of the industrial revolution the rich mineral deposits, especially salt, became more important, and eventually textile, chemical and metallurgical plants were established. More recently oil discoveries have added significantly to the region's economic well-being and prosperity.

Czernowitz, today known as Chernovtsy, was an ancient city which has paid allegiance to many flags. During the Middle Ages it was under the rule of the Russian principality of Kiev, and from the fourteenth to the seventeenth centuries was a part of Poland. Austria captured the city in 1774, made it the capital of Bucovina and controlled it until World War I. For a time it was granted to Rumania, but Russia seized it toward the end of World War II and it is today the capital of the Chernovtsy region of the USSR.

In 1904, the year the Rosenstocks and the Ashenbergs left for America, Jewish emigration from Europe was nearing its peak. Until the 1870s, Jewish departures were predominantly from the United Kingdom, Germany, and Scandinavia, with the shift to central and eastern Europe starting in the late nineteenth century.

The Jews had few friends among the leaders of the European countries, the exceptions being Napoleon Bonaparte and Francis Joseph I. Wherever Napoleon's armies appeared, the walls of the Jewish ghettos fell. Influenced by Napoleon, a new consistorial organization was established in 1808, with consistories formed in every community where there were more than 2,000 Jews. The synagogue was assigned the responsibility of providing for Jewish conscription.

Following the defeat of Prussia and the Third Coalition, Napoleon provided numerous freedoms and rights to the Jews. Special taxes were abolished, Jews were granted full citizenship in several countries and all types of economic enterprise were opened to them. But Napoleon's reign came to an end at Waterloo, setting loose all of the anti-Semitic forces that had, at the least, been held in check. The fate of the Jews varied from country to country. The old restrictions reappeared in Germany almost immediately. In Frankfurt, the ghetto was re-established as soon as French control had disappeared. Lubeck and Bremen expelled most of their Jews within weeks and deprived the others of all civil and political rights.

The Jewish lot in Austria rapidly deteriorated. By paying a special tax, certain Jews were permitted to live in Vienna and visiting Jews had a maximum of fourteen days to conduct their business. In Italy the Inquisition was once again put into effect and all rights were taken from the Jews, attendance at the Cathedral of Saint Angelo to hear a missionary address by a priest was compulsory, and each year the Jews had to pay their taxes in a carnival ceremony, dressed as clowns.

Another temporary interlude in the anti-Semitic battle occurred in the mid-nineteenth century during the regency of William I in Germany and Francis Joseph I in Austria. In Germany Jews were identified with every important enterprise and became a significant element of the *bourgeoisie*. In Austria they were decreed eligible for all positions and eventually were admitted into hereditary nobility. Francis Joseph I came to the throne when he was eighteen (in 1848) and served until 1916. Politically he was conservative, conciliatory, encouraging a more temperate attitude toward the Jews and eliminating the pogroms against the Yiddish people that frequently led to riots and often bloody massacres. Selig recalled that he was instructed by his elders to remember the Emperor in his prayers and was told to ask for a continuation of his already long and eventful reign.

It was, at best, an uneasy truce. The clericals and aristocrats in Austria had never accepted the *Ausgleich* of 1867, and after the financial crisis of 1873 the attacks against Jews became more frequent and more violent. After anti-Semite forces took control of the municipal council of Vienna in 1895, installing Karl Lueger, a fanatic Jew-hater, as burgomaster, outbreaks became almost continuous. Jews made attempts to remove the anti-Semite faction from power by allying themselves with liberal movements, but their position remained insecure. Even such assimilationists as Theodor Herzl, the founder of modern political Zionism, published *The Jewish State* in 1896, renouncing his former belief that the future of the Jews lay in complete absorption in European life. At a Jewish congress in 1897 he declared that "the object of Zionism is to establish for the Jewish people a publicly and legally assured home in Palestine." At the time, large segments of the Jewish people disagreed, never dreaming that he would turn out to be a remarkable prophet.

Under such circumstances and with a foreboding of things to come if they were to remain in Europe, the Rosenstocks and Ashenbergs made final preparations, selling virtually everything they owned, bringing to America only those personal necessities and a few precious memorabilia that were too close to one's heart to leave behind.

There were few goodbyes since the entire family was leaving, with the exception of Selig's Aunt Golda Ashenberg who had left Galicia years before to live in Russia. She came to Czernowitz for the final embrace and Selig recalled: "She was a beautiful woman, and I was quite impressed with her. She stayed with us a few days, trying to ease some of the bittersweet pain. There was pain of sorts, leaving a land our families had known for so many generations. She returned to Russia and was involved in the Russian Revolution of 1905. We never heard from her again and assume she was killed in Russia, as so many Jews were."

And so it was, in the early fall of 1904, that Grandmother Ashenberg, Leah Rosenstock and her two children, Selig and Anne, and Selig's Aunt Ada and Uncle Zigmund Kremnitz left Czernowitz for Hamburg, Germany, the departure point for America. It was not Uncle Zigmund's limousine that carried them this time to the familiar railroad station. Selig Usher Rosenstock, age nine, was en route to the "home of the brave and the land of the free," not only to find a new life, but a new name as well. He would soon be subjected to Americanization in American schools and would be advised by the teacher who enrolled him that Selig was not a proper name for a boy in this country, and he would be arbitrarily christened Fred Asher Rosenstock, officially and for all time.

Hamburg, one of the three primary emigration ports at that time (along with Bremen, Germany, and Rotterdam, Holland), was about a thousand miles northwest of Czernowitz. The railroad generally followed the Dniester River to Drogobych, crossing the Carpathian and Sudeten mountains into Poland, through Berlin, finally reaching the valley of the River Elbe for the last two hundred miles to Hamburg.

To Fred Rosenstock it was a time of great excitement. His face was constantly creased with a smile, his childish countenance one of awe, his eyes glued to the train windows as vista after vista unfolded. His questions to his mother and Uncle Zigmund were endless and, for the most part, unanswered.

The city of Hamburg was an inland port, situated on the northern branch of the Elbe about 55 miles from the North Sea port of Cuxhaven. One of the most important trade centers of Europe, Hamburg is crisscrossed with canals (*Fleeten*) which serve as water highways for freight. Originally founded by Charlemagne (in the ninth century), who built a citadel and a church on the heights between the Elbe and the east bank of the Alster, the city has a fascinating array of historic landmarks.

From almost any point in the city tall church spires can be seen rising above the skyline, edifices built in the fourteenth, fifteenth and seventeenth centuries.

"I remember the streets in Hamburg — the canal running right through the center of this long street — with flowers on each side, masses of flowers as far as my eyes could see." It was here, Fred reminisced, that he had his first taste of chocolates. "We were in Hamburg for about four days before the ship left, and we made a lot of friends, mostly with others who were taking the trip. One particular man impressed me, and I guess I impressed him. He wanted me to see Hamburg, and my mother agreed to let me go with him. I held his hand and started looking, my eyes like saucers. We must have spent an entire afternoon sightseeing in the center section of the city. He must have had the same love for books as my Uncle Morris, for we went into many different bookstores. Even then bookstores had a fascination for me. Toward the end of the afternoon we stepped into one shop and he bought a box of chocolates. In Biala Potok, and even in Czernowitz, I never had chocolates. It was always hard candy, and not very much of that, either. Anyway, that was the first time I had ever eaten a piece of chocolate, and I thought it was pretty good."

The day for sailing finally arrived, and the Rosenstock-Ashenberg entourage joined with hundreds of others to board the passenger liner *Patrizia,* a high-funneled, long and sleek German ship. It is probable that one of the reasons for the great exodus from Europe to America during the latter part of the nineteenth century was the rapid development of steam vessels, which had been substantially improved since the day that Fulton's paddle-wheeler made its historic trip up the Hudson in 1807. By 1819 the first American ship, the *Savannah,* had made the trans-oceanic voyage from Savannah, Georgia, to Liverpool, England, in twenty-seven days, eighty hours of which were under steam power.

The early journeys were precarious. One vessel, the *Arctic,* was lost in a collision off Cape Race in 1854; the *Pacific* sailed from Liverpool on September 23, 1856 and was never heard from again; the *Atlantic* was destroyed at sea in 1871; and the *Baltic* was lost in 1880. Until the 1880s, steam engines were considered as auxiliary power and most ships flew canvas to reassure passengers.

But the *Patrizia* had no sails and those who boarded her that day in 1904 were in a festive mood, standing on the top deck and waving good-byes to friends, relatives, and others who merely came to watch the great blackhulled ship start on its way up the Elbe. By late afternoon the *Patrizia* had reached Cuxhaven and was at the mouth of the open sea.

The first and only port-of-call was Queenstown, Ireland. After a twenty-four-hour layover to take on fuel and supplies, the *Patrizia* headed west into the North Atlantic.

In Fred Rosenstock's words: "There were emigrants from all over Europe, and, of course, even in those days there were great differences in the clothes the people from different countries wore. Russia and Austria — at least the part from which I came and which eventually became Russia — were very close together geographically, but the clothes and customs were miles apart.

"There were quite a few Russians on the ship, real Russian *muzhiks* — peasant farmers. They were primitive, sort of wild and crude, and wearing high cossack boots. I especially remember the boots because of what happened aboard ship. We had second-class passage, but at certain times everyone would be on deck, and the crew — German sailors — would pass out salted herrings. Most of the passengers would take one or two, but the Russians grabbed handful after handful, and when they couldn't hold any more would stuff them in their boots. They would eat them off and on for the rest of the day. I think they subsisted on a fish diet for the whole trip."

As second-class passengers, the Ashenbergs and Rosenstocks didn't have individual cabins, but slept below in a large dormitory arrangement, with rows of upper and lower berths offering a minimum of privacy. But it did tend to foster fraternization, and there were many conversations about the New World. Although there were many different nationalities — Germans, Austrians, Poles, Czechs — and many different languages, communication was never a problem. All had a common bond and all shared the same enthusiasm for the exciting life ahead of them. Fred always had a smile and was interested in everything and everybody. From time to time, to the pleasure of the other passengers, he would sing Jewish hymns in his clear, high voice.

For the most part it was a happy voyage, with much singing and dancing. Food was served communally at long tables and when the dinner was over the passengers would join the crew in singing German songs, and the sailors would seek out the attractive young women and dance the night away to the music of a small German band.

During the two-week voyage only one day of stormy weather was encountered, with the captain ordering all passengers to remain below deck. For a young boy, the experience of looking out a porthole and seeing nothing but water was frightening, and a few fearful tears were shed as Fred found solace in his mother's arms. The emigrants were not only of all nationalities, but all ages as well. Some were babes still in arms, some were old, some infirm. And there was death on the voyage, making a depressing but indelible mark on Fred Rosenstock's consciousness as he watched the body being placed in a weighted canvas bag and lowered into the ocean to be swallowed by the waves.

Finally, the end of the journey. Word spread like a sudden wind throughout the ship that land would soon be in sight and the passengers rushed to the deck, all wanting to be the first to glimpse the shoreline of America. Emotions were no longer kept inside as tears of hope flowed freely and dreams of a brighter tomorrow came into view.

CHAPTER VI

ROMANCE & REAL ESTATE

THROUGHOUT FRED ROSENSTOCK'S LONG LIFE, he has frequently referred to "miracles" that have played a vital role both in his business career and his personal history. Perhaps some of the events were miracles, by his definition, but they were hardly supernatural. In retrospect, most of the "miraculous" things happened as the result of Fred's facility for making the most of his opportunities and his talents.

He had met the real estate entrepreneur Joseph DeRose many months before the demise of the Denver Book Shop, and it was no miracle that DeRose liked what he saw in the young and ambitious Rosenstock; a man with a quick smile and a warm and outgoing personality that were natural attributes of a supersalesman. DeRose was also aware of Fred's experience in business. So it was no miracle that the astute realtor offered Fred a forty-sixty partnership in his firm.

"My association with DeRose was a mixture of fun and business," Fred relates, "and sometimes it seemed to me that it was mostly fun. Joe was one of a family of nine children whose parents had emigrated from Potenza, Italy, early in the century and settled in the semi-agricultural Italian-American colony in Welby, just north of Denver. For a country boy, Joe had made a rapid advance in the real estate business, and was the hail-fellow-well-met type among his own people as well as many others in the business world of that time. Joe worked hard when he worked, but he also wasted a lot of time. I must admit (though it didn't occur to me then) that I was also wasting my time; in fact, I was in a kind of happy lethargy and enjoying it.

[65]

"Prohibition was still in effect, and Joe knew all the 'spots.' He and I tarried in some rather torrid places of the day. I even got to know some of the more famous (and infamous) characters of the time. Joe considered himself a pretty good billiard player and many an afternoon he would take off for Tony Sarconi's Billiard Parlor — it was actually a betting parlor — and end up losing all the money he had on him, as well as missing all his appointments."

Fred's heart was still, as it would always be, in the book business, and the more time that Joe DeRose spent at Sarconi's, the more time Fred spent hunting for books, his thoughts becoming ever stronger about re-entering the book field. But he made the most of his years with DeRose, and met some interesting personalities. "Our real estate office," he recalls, "was on the third floor of the Central Savings Bank Building in downtown Denver. It was actually a suite of several rooms which we shared with another real estate man, A. E. Sponsler, who had a profitable sideline — signing up new members for the Woodmen of the World, for which he received a commission of so much a head.

"We had the prestige of having a public stenographer in our office — and she was quite a character. She was her own boss and told off anybody and everybody when she felt like it — except A. E. Sponsler who, in her eyes, could do no wrong. He was a man of elegance and bearing, down to his perfumed handkerchief and clipped English accent. Quite a personality!

"One time, I was sitting in the office waiting for someone to come in who never did show up. I was getting a bit sleepy, in fact, when a character walked in who had me a bit startled. He was old, small and wiry, with a kind of furtive look — like a detective. And indeed, that's what he turned out to be — an old-time, retired detective and one of the old Wild West types at that! He was asking our opinionated public stenographer, Hattie Osborn, if she was a public stenographer. He talked low, but I strained my ears. He wanted to know if she could type a script from notes he had relating some of his past experiences.

"She announced emphatically that she could type anything. He began to pull out little slips of paper, with handwritten scratchings on them, from all pockets, and put them together like puzzle sheets. Finally Miss Osborn began to type, with this mysterious stranger looking over her shoulder.

"The going was slow, and she had difficulty reading his writing, so she would ask him from time to time, 'What's this?' or 'What do you mean here?' I was wide awake now, leaning forward to hear his every word. I was really becoming interested since I began to realize that this man was talking *history,* and in fact had been one of the makers of history. I'll keep you in suspense no longer. This was Doc Shores, the famous western lawman who ran down and captured some of the most desperate criminals in Colorado and New Mexico. And there I was, listening to his own story in his own words! For many years after, I wondered what had happened to the manuscript which Miss Osborn typed up. The answer is to be found in the book entitled, *Memoirs of a Lawman,* by Wilson Rockwell, published by Swallow Press and still in print.

"Across the hall from us was another interesting office. It was a small room and everything in it, the furniture, the rug, and the two occupants, were all of ancient vintage — dating back I would say to the 1880s. One of the occupants was William G. Evans, son of one of Colorado's most famous governors for whom Mount Evans was named. William G. himself was president of the Denver Tramway Company, a bank director and quite a business titan in the Mile-High City. The other man with him was a study in contrasts. It was his cousin, Howard Evans, who looked more like an ivory-tower professor than a business tycoon.

"I might have been more awed by such men of power had I known who they really were and what they represented, but to me they were just two nice old men, and I liked them that way. William G. would notice me walking down the hall and would hail me. 'Come in, young man, I'd like to talk to you.' I would tell him about some of my daily doings and about books, and he listened attentively. I often remembered with regret that I didn't ask him more questions about himself or discuss some of the historical facets I am sure he could have related to me.

"Another person of more than ordinary interest had offices on an upper floor, and I got to know him rather well as he, too, would bring in work for Miss Osborn to do. This was Vaso Chucovich, who, with Ed Chase, reportedly owned the biggest gambling operation in Denver at the turn of the century. At the time I knew him, Chucovich had long since retired from his early occupations. He appeared as a refined and distinguished-looking gentleman, and to me had a very grandfatherly and almost condescending manner. Some years later, when Chucovich died, his huge fortune was distributed, the main portion going to relatives in Serbia, the land of his birth."

While Fred Rosenstock was marking time, adding slowly and carefully to his private book collection between real estate transactions and waiting for the day when he would again become a book dealer, life in America was bouncing along in an era of postwar prosperity, prohibition and speakeasies. A tired President Warren G. Harding looked on in disbelief as the Teapot Dome scandal took over the headlines and his Attorney General, Harry F. Daugherty, and his Secretary of the Interior, Albert B. Fall, were found to be deeply involved in one of the most spectacular frauds in government — not to be surpassed until the Watergate scandal of the 1970s.

It was a time for isolationism, nationalism, and growing bigotry. The Ku Klux Klan was revived, and grew from one hundred thousand members in 1919 to an estimated six million by the end of 1924. So great was its political influence that it forced the defeat of a resolution condemning Klan activities at the Democratic National Convention.

The Klan moved into Colorado in 1920 and claimed thirty thousand white-sheeted members under the leadership of Galen Locke. As on the national scene, the "Kolorado Klavern" exerted considerable political influence. In the 1924 elections they virtually took over the city and state, controlled the legislature, and dictated most of the appointments that were made, particularly in the police department. At one point the Klan actually controlled a majority of the the judges in the Denver District Court, according to Ida Libert Uchill, noted historian of the Jews in Colorado.

In his book, *The First Hundred Years* (Doubleday, 1959), Robert L. Perkin notes that the Kolorado Klavern didn't have much in common with the Southern branch. Its persecution of Jews, Catholics, Negroes and Spanish-Americans was economic and social rather than physical. Crosses were burned on top of Table Mountain and Ruby Hill, but no killings or lynchings were ever proved.

Fred, being a Jew, had no love for the KKK. Recalling this period in the twenties, he relates that "the air became thick with dissension and distrust. Longtime friendships were cooled or shaken, and overall there was a feeling of fear. Jobs were lost for no evident reason, salesmen were given cold treatment by faithful customers, and I personally remember clearly some of my Jewish and Catholic friends being worried as to their personal safety.

"The Klan had a fiery cross burning nightly on a mountain in the Golden foothills, and although I had not encountered any serious problems myself, I could not escape the foreboding atmosphere. For example, I considered myself a close friend of the Denver booksellers of the time, was one of their intimate circle, played poker with them, socialized with them. Even in this limited group, I began to feel the impact of the 'disease.'

"I recall attending a big protest or 'defense' meeting at the City Auditorium, packed to the rafters, and hearing fervent speeches by Father McMenamin of the Cathedral, Rabbi William S. Friedman of the Jewish Temple, and others. The head of the Klan in Colorado was an M.D., Dr. Galen Locke, who was a paradox in some ways. Even though he was the Grand Dragon or Grand Kleagle, he still cared medically for the many Italian patients who represented a large part of his practice.

"The only actual experience I had with the Klan was rather humorous; at least, that's how it struck me at the time. Practically across the street from the Central Savings building was a restaurant where I would go for lunch. It was close by, and the food was good. Rumors were afloat that the owner was a 'Kluxer,' and that this restaurant was a sort of meeting place of the Klan. I didn't let this bother me and continued to eat there.

"One noon, as was my custom, I sat down at the counter and had given my order when the owner (with whom I'd never before had any conversation) sidled up facing me, and began to speak in a rather easy but subtle way, asking me questions about myself. He said he had noticed me as a steady customer — and thanked me for this — and after I gave him my name, he asked, 'You're Jewish, aren't you?' I said, 'Yes.' He then, in a soft and beguiling manner, said something like, 'You are probably aware that this restaurant caters to a certain group,' and he followed it up with a remark like, 'We don't really hate Jews,' but then came the bullet! He said, 'Wouldn't you, yourself, feel more at home if you ate at another place?' I took the hint and held my cool (I complimented myself on the manner in which I acted out my part). I said, 'Yes, you're right. I agree I would feel better somewhere else.'

"Dissensions within the Klan, exposure of its pressures and underground methods, and also the corrupt practices of some of its higher-ups, finally caused the Klan to evaporate. At this point, it was somewhat amusing to me when certain old friends began to 'confess' to me that they had been Klan members, and there were apologies and heartbeatings no end. And so we came back to normalcy, as I believe President Harding used to say.

"In 1924, other things were happening in Denver. The campaign, '500,000 by 1930' was flaunted on banners all up and down Sixteenth and Seventeenth streets. That fizzled, as it was bound to. By now we know better than to try to balloon population by ballyhoo. Population grows without any help, even when we don't need it. This was several years before the depression, but Denver got an early taste of what it was going to be like. Several bank closings shook the city, and there were many individual sufferings. The Hibernia Bank, the Home Savings and Trust, and the Italian-American Bank all failed.

"The sad circumstance of the Italian-American Bank disaster was brought home to me closely, because so many of the Italian-American population who lost their money knew my partner DeRose and would come to our office — some in tears — wondering if 'Joe could do anything for them.' It was really pitiful. Some people lost lifetime savings, the result of years of hard labor and frugality. One Italian-American — a truck gardener — came in to see Joe, and Joe happened to be out. The man was frantic over his loss. But what was funny, in a way, was that he did not seem to mind so much losing the $15,000 principal as the fact that he had been dilatory and hadn't drawn the interest, as had been his practice for years."

Early indicators of a weakening economy in 1926 went virtually unnoticed. The automobile and construction industries had peaked, and, in Denver, population growth had leveled off and the real estate business had started a slow decline. Joe DeRose began spending more time at Sarconi's, and Fred started spending more time looking for books.

"Someone told me to go to Central City," he relates, "which was really a ghost town at that time, and said I could find houses that had been abandoned years before and where people had left things, particularly books, which could be had for the taking.

"So one Sunday morning I invited a girl I had met to go with me. She was a Denver girl, but had never been to Central City. We took the Colorado Central train and got there on a sunny, warm, summer's day. We barely met a living person on the streets. And the story was true — abandoned houses were wide open, and there *were* books lying about. I could not carry any large quantities with me, but I did corral a few rare items which I brought back to Denver."

Until this period in Fred's life, he had become romantically involved only once, with Jeannette Stadler. He dated the girl he had taken to Central City occasionally, but had no serious intentions about her, or anyone else. Their relationship ended when she urged him to consider a more permanent arrangement. He was nearly thirty, mature, personable, and financially solvent. But his ambitions had not been fulfilled, and he felt that love would have to wait. In fact, he had not met the right girl.

In Fred's words, "I was so deeply immersed in my enthusiasm for books, with history, and with an inner feeling that I was getting somewhere in my newly adopted city, that any ideas of marriage or settling down, so to speak, were outside my realm of thought." But fate, or in Fred's words, "the greatest miracle" of his life, changed his ideas. "Suppose," he says, "I had left DeRose and the Central Savings Bank building — my whole life would have been something else. This was 1924, and by then I knew most of the people in the building, enough to say hello to, at least. But one day, while passing through the hallway of our own floor, I saw a young girl who looked about eighteen or nineteen, with black hair and beautiful black eyes. I glanced at her and smiled, but that was all. That wasn't really all. Somehow she would appear and reappear in my thoughts, and I kept hoping I would see her again. I wondered who she was and if she worked in the building. I did pass by her once or twice, just for a fleeting moment, but finally there was a lucky break. It was the end of the day, and I entered the elevator, and there she was, also leaving. She had a number of small packages in her arms, and all of a sudden one little package dropped to the floor. I picked it up quickly, gave it to her, and she said 'thanks' with an electrifying smile. I still didn't know who she was, but I did know that I was going to find out. At least now I could say 'hello' and get a 'hello' back.

"A few questions the next day and I knew her name was Frances Goodman and that she worked for a dentist in the building, lived on Stuart Street on the west side, was one of six children, and that her father was a tailor with a shop in the old Railroad building. After a few more chance encounters in the hallways, I decided to ask her to a dance. That was something I was pretty good at, and in those days there were nice public dance halls. One of my favorites was the Columbine Hall at Colfax and Clarkson, now occupied by the Denver Turnverein.

"But it wasn't as easy as I had hoped. She turned me down politely, explaining that she was finishing her high school education by attending evening classes at Manual High five nights a week. 'What about Saturday?' I asked.

" 'On Saturday,' she said, ' I help my mother with the younger children.'

" 'What about Sunday?' I persisted, and this time I got another kind of answer, a little on the chilling side, I have to say.

" 'I have a steady date on Sundays.'

"It looked like no openings anywhere. 'You mean *every* Sunday?' I asked.

" 'Yes, every Sunday,' was her reply. Even her smile didn't help.

"I was unhappy, to say the least, but I went through the motions and said, 'Well, I'll keep asking you. Maybe something will change.'

"And I did. I asked her to dances, to a show, to the theatre. Denver had some good theatre in those days, and I was a frequent patron at the Broadway where Peter McCourt, elder brother of Baby Doe Tabor, took tickets. And shows — what shows! The great musicals, the Ziegfeld Follies, Al Jolson, Eddie Cantor, and the other famous names played the Broadway. Denver was on the regular circuit; you didn't have to wait six months for a good show to come around. If you wanted to see a good play, the Denham Players, with Gladys George, George Barnes, Ben Erway and the rest were nearly always delightful. As far as theatre is concerned in Denver, I miss the good old days.

"But I had my own drama going, and I began to wonder if it was to have a happy ending. Finally one day the heavens opened and she said, 'When?' I knew there must have been a change somewhere, somehow, but I didn't ask questions or worry about reasons. For me it was a windfall!"

Over the next several weeks, Fred dated her as often as she would let him, and she was as delightful and charming as he had imagined she would be. He met her family and her five brothers and sisters — three of whom were younger than Frances. "The younger kids, in particular, took to me. On those evenings when they knew I was coming, they would sit on the curbstone at the corner of West Colfax and Stuart, meet me alighting from the streetcar and romp with me the block and a half to the house.

"I would bring them presents — little things — and sometimes before even letting Frances know I was there the kids would capture me for a ballgame right on the street. This happened more than once, and sometimes, because of it, I'd be late. Frances would look out the window and see me playing with the boys and say, half-joking, 'Who do you come to see, the kids or me?'

"I cannot adequately describe my happiness over the succeeding months. Despite the difference in our ages (Frances was nineteen and Fred about thirty), we seemed supremely suited to each other. Great times — dances, shows, picnics, short trips to places like Eldorado Springs, Grand Lake, Glenwood, and Colorado Springs — were the order of the day, and sometimes we would take the kids along. It surely appeared that I was in love, not merely with a girl, but with a family!"

Frances was, naturally, very much interested in her boyfriend's business career, and it didn't take her long to perceive that Fred's ambition was to get back in the book business. "Her encouragement was so sincere and prevailing that I could not help feeling that I had someone who *really* cared.

"I had not yet proposed to her. In fact, there was really never a proposal as such. We mutually took things for granted. We had many talks about my future, and her comments and advice impressed upon me that whatever I should turn to, I could be assured of a great companion and partner — which she actually did become — for most of the years of my life."

It has been said that to be successful one must *think* "success." To Fred Rosenstock, opportunity was the key word in his philosophy. He *thought* "opportunity," and consequently he had more knocks on his door than the adage prescribes. By the spring of 1925 his romance had blossomed along with the columbine and the daffodils, and he was thinking of ways to make extra money, knowing that he would soon have some additional responsibilities — and also feeling a strong urge to return to the book business, a venture which would require substantial capital.

"In those days," Fred recalls, "the Fourth of July was celebrated vigorously, and on the night of the Fourth every home with children resounded with fireworks of all kinds, from sparklers to cannon crackers, Roman candles, and all the rest. I conceived an idea of going into the fireworks business in a big way for a two-week period — a week for preparation, a second week for business and a clean-up at the end. First of all, I obtained the fireworks, and was lucky enough to get the goods on consignment from three different wholesale jobbers — which gave me the most complete assortment of anybody in town. Then I had about twenty thousand discount cards printed, which I distributed among large employers such as Gates Rubber Company, Shwayder Brothers (makers of Samsonite luggage), Public Service, and Mountain Bell. When these cards were shown to our cashier at the time of purchase the customer would receive a twenty percent discount. I rented a vacant store in a top downtown location, hired high school help — and did a land-office business. I kept up this fireworks business in later years, at one time having as many as six locations at once in downtown Denver. Some of these 'fireworks kids' who worked for me developed into people of note and became leading citizens of Denver.

"Frances was enthusiastic about the enterprise and helped me greatly. At all times we seemed to feel we were doing it not just for *me* but for *us*. We became as one in our hopes and interests. One day, in a very natural way, I said to her, 'Suppose we select an engagement ring?' I can't recall what she said, but she was agreeable. So we bought a ring, and within a matter of days we announced our engagement.

"We originally planned a large wedding, but almost ended up having a funeral instead. About three weeks before the date we had set, I ate a hot dog sandwich at a place called Joy's Sandwich Shop (it was at Sixteenth and Arapahoe) — and it resulted in no joy at all. I contracted ptomaine poisoning and was rushed to St. Luke's Hospital. The poisoning reached the point of causing me to lose consciousness. I almost went into a coma and the doctors hovered about me, not sure if I would live or die. Anyway, the good Lord and the good doctors prevailed — and I remember that when I opened my eyes, there was my sweetheart standing over me. I recuperated quickly, but we changed our plans for the big wedding and were married on a Sunday morning, June 6, 1926, on the lawn outside her parents' home.

"For our honeymoon, we decided to rent a cabin on a high mountain overlooking Manitou, a resort town near Colorado Springs. We were there two weeks. My wife would go shopping at Manitou and then practice cooking on me.

"I thought while we were so close to Colorado Springs it might be worthwhile to advertise for books — private libraries, Western Americana, fine bindings — so I framed an ad to run in the *Colorado Springs Gazette*. I was still recuperating from my spell of ptomaine poisoning, so after the ad had run several days Frances went to the newspaper office to pick up any possible replies. She returned with a large batch, mostly uninteresting and hardly worth pursuing. However, she did have an interesting experience at the newspaper office. When she called for the replies she was waited on by an elderly man, a Mr. Connor, dressed 'old-style' with a straight-up wing collar, but nevertheless elegantly attired in the fashion of the 1890s. He asked about the ad and she told him that her husband was a rare book dealer and that we were on our honeymoon.

"He was friendly and talkative, and revealed that he had been a close friend of Robert Louis Stevenson years ago, and in fact had visited with Stevenson and his wife at their last home in Samoa. He said further that when they parted the Stevensons gave him about fifty books from their library — mostly first editions, and all bearing autographs. Frances asked if he still had those books, and he said yes, in his apartment in Colorado Springs. We ended up going to his place and purchasing the collection. It was a thrill to own those books, all personal relics of the Stevensons — but as it happened I didn't enjoy the ownership very long.

"John Howell, the noted San Francisco rare book dealer, unexpectedly came to Denver and paid me a visit. I really did not want to

Fred and Frances shortly after their marriage

dispose of these Stevenson books — at least, not so soon, but Howell persisted and I gave in. I turned them over at such a minimal profit that, as
I recall, it provoked the first tongue-lashing I received from my wife."

Fred's relationship with Joseph DeRose was on a part-time basis, and
both he and Frances began looking around for a location suitable for a
bookstore. But an unexpected opportunity developed that would delay
the western bookman from pursuing his destiny.

CHAPTER VII

DREAMS TO REALITY

IT WAS NO LONGER "FRED ROSENSTOCK." For the next forty-six years, it would be "The Rosenstocks," Fred and Frances. And Frances understood her husband, his talents as well as his ambitions. Even more important, she shared these ambitions and became an integral part of Fred Rosenstock's life, as wife, companion, business associate, and confidante.

Following the abbreviated honeymoon in Manitou, they moved into a modest apartment at 2330 Glenarm, convenient to the downtown area but with few aesthetic attributes. For the next year, Fred continued to put in some time with DeRose, waiting for the opportunity to become a book dealer once more. Shortly after his marriage, he bid his bride goodbye and took off on one of his many trips east for the purpose of building the collection that he would ultimately need for his bookstore, wherever it might be.

By the early summer of 1927 Fred had accumulated a collection of first editions that included significant holdings of representative American and English authors. It was time, Fred and Frances agreed, to take some positive steps toward their new career. Remembering his previous debacle with the Denver Book Shop, Fred was determined to have sufficient capital to insure the success of his next bookstore venture. To accumulate cash, he commenced discussions with the Anderson Galleries of New York City in August, 1927, relative to the sale at auction of his collection of first editions.

With the books he had held back from the first auction at the Denver Book Shop, and the buying and trading he had continued to do throughout the first half of the twenties, his library consisted of several thousand volumes. Few books were kept at the Glenarm apartment, with most of his collection in cartons and on bookshelves in the family home at 208 Twenty-fourth Street, where his parents had moved after eight months in the place Fred had originally rented for them on Gilpin Street. The quantity of books cluttered the house, but Fred's mother was always pleased to have them, knowing that as long as the books were there her son would be a frequent visitor.

Once negotiations with Anderson Galleries had been completed, a sale catalog was published, including 708 separate listings and a total of thirteen hundred volumes. The preface read: "First Editions of Modern Authors — George Ade, T. B. Aldrich, Max Beerbohm, Ambrose Bierce, James Branch Cabell, Willa Cather, S. L. Clemens, Joseph Conrad, Stephen Crane, Theodore Dreiser, Richard Le Gallienne, Jack London, Amy Lowell, John Masefield, Herman Melville, H. L. Mencken, George Moore, Edward Arlington Robinson, Theodore Roosevelt, Edgar Saltus, R. L. Stevenson, Henry D. Thoreau, Walt Whitman, Oscar Wilde, and many others, with a few older authors, collected by Fred A. Rosenstock, Denver, Colorado. . . ." An impressive list, and one which catapulted the young Jewish immigrant into the hierarchy of American bibliophiles.

Fred Rosenstock did more than merely collect books. He studied the volumes, becoming an expert as far as the content was concerned as well as a connoisseur of the physical attributes of fine and rare books. It was this knowledge and his perfectionist attitude toward books that led to strong disagreements between Fred and the Anderson Galleries.

The auction was set for December 12, 1927, at two o'clock in the afternoon and at eight-fifteen in the evening. The date was of great concern to him, since the American Art Association was holding a sale that would be in direct conflict.

When Fred received the catalog on December 6, he wrote a fiery letter to William H. Smith, Jr., vice president of the Gallery. He said, in part, "I have all along . . . tried to impress certain main features of the

sale, both upon Mr. Kingsland (with whom he had originally nego-
tiated, and who subsequently left Anderson Galleries and went to the
American Art Association) and yourself, and it now appears — much
as I hate to say it — that in almost every one of these matters, it has
developed contrary to my hopes and desires.

"First and most damaging is the fact that the sale will be held at the
same time and on the same day that the American Art Association will
hold a competitive sale. Only recently I expressed my fear of the occur-
rence of such a thing, and your letter of November 21 in reply states
'there is no occasion for any anxiety concerning your sale, and our date
will be entirely clear of any conflicting date at the American Art Association.' In view of this, you can agree that it is a distinct shock to me.
... The least that you could have done would have been to paste a new
date slip on the catalogues, just as you did with a recent sale on which
the dates conflicted.

"The consolidation is excessive — much more than I had expected.
However, that is not nearly so bad a fault as the fact that the catalogue is
full of errors, in nearly every case to my disadvantage. I am not at all
finicky, but I am in business myself, and rebel at apparent sheer negli-
gence no matter who perpetrates it. I will not dwell upon details at this
time, but am enclosing a list of 'corrections and suggestions,' which I do
sincerely hope will be given attention previous to and at the sale. ...

"Another criticism I believe I am just in making is that although the
most minute little defects have been brought out to such an extent that I
cannot, frankly, recall an equal to it; it appears that very small mention,
comparatively, was made of the good points relating to various items,
such as 'fine copies' or listing books 'new in dust jacket.' The latter description is used so much in auction catalogues that it astonishes me im-
mensely that it was not at all used in my list."

Smith defended his position by stressing that, in his opinion, the sale
at the American Art Association would not conflict with the Rosenstock
sale. "It is," he wrote, "of a totally different character from yours, and
the people who would be interested in yours would not be interested in

theirs, and vice versa. . . . With regard to the mention of defects in your catalogue . . . I want to say that I felt such mention was absolutely necessary in order to prevent the return of books by purchasers if they were not mentioned. You had very many books with names of former owners on fly-leaves. That must be constituted a defect, especially among what may be termed 'collectors' books . . . I trust that with all your criticisms the sale will be financially to your satisfaction, and we shall do what we can in the selling to have it so."

The sale brought about half of what Mr. Kingsland had estimated at the preliminary discussions with Fred Rosenstock, and naturally the Denver book collector was extremely disappointed. He raised several questions concerning the handling of the sale, to which Anderson Galleries responded: "Please dismiss from your mind the idea that the sale at the American Art Association in any way interfered with yours. The attendance was HERE. Mr. Drake was here in person; Dr. Rosenbach was represented; Brick Row Book Shop was represented, as well as many others, including some new private buyers.

"The fault lay, to my way of thinking, in the character of the authors collected. Nobody today collects Louisa M. Alcott; John Kendrick Bangs; H. C. Bunner; Madison Cawein; Le Gallienne; and others I might mention, and of others the priced catalogue will tell you plainly that only the scarcest of their books are sought for. In these days the collector does not strive to obtain ALL the books any certain author has written, but only the rarest, and most desirable, consequently the minor books go for a song."

John T. Winterich, in his book *Collector's Choice,* apparently refers to the sale of the Rosenstock collection: "The day of the sale arrives; the auctioneer mounts the rostrum with no greater fanfare than if he were putting out the cat, announces in a hurried formula that this is the library of Mr. X of Xville, calls attention to the conditions of sale, and almost before the audience has settled into its seats is through with Lot Number One.

"Lot Number One is an assortment of ten first editions of George

Ade, from *Artie* (1896) to *Hand-Made Fables* (1920). If Mr. X bought the books new, as he doubtless did buy some of them, the lot probably cost him a minimum of ten dollars. It sells for five. There are a few things by Louisa May Alcott, including a presentation copy of her first book, *Flower Fables* (1855), which brings five dollars — *this must be one of the occasional bargain days in the auction room.*

"There are half a dozen or so items of Thomas Bailey Aldrich, including seventeen of John Kendrick Bangs in a lot (including one presentation copy — the lot goes for eight dollars), some Barries and Beerbohms, a good run of books by Ambrose Bierce, twenty or so Cabells, several Clemenses, Conrads, and Cranes. And so on — it were profitless to exhaust the alphabet."

Whether this is a true representation or not, Fred was bitterly disappointed. The results, as he wrote Mr. Smith, were a debacle, and for a time he gave serious consideration to a thorough investigation of the way the sale was handled, and possible legal action. His irritation increased when he learned that a fellow collector had attempted to buy certain lots of the books listed in the Rosenstock sales catalog but had not received them — the lots going to other bidders for less than his offer. However, Fred eventually took the advice of one of his old book dealer friends, accepted his losses and looked to the future instead of the past.

At about the time he entered in negotiations with Anderson Galleries — August 1927 — most of the conversation at the Rosenstock house revolved around the topic of starting a new bookstore. Fred and Frances spent many hours searching the want ads and visiting various locations that offered possibilities.

An unexpected development occurred that temporarily deferred their plans. Perhaps, with the Anderson Gallery sale being less profitable than they had hoped, it was another of the Rosenstock "miracles" that postponed the opening of their bookstore.

It was mid-summer, and Fred had parted company (on friendly

terms) with Joe DeRose, when he received a phone call from Fred Forrester, one of the leading insurance agents in Denver, who represented several of the old-line companies. His clients included many of the city's largest firms at that time, and Forrester had about twenty agents affiliated with him throughout the state.

"He wanted me to come to his office. I didn't know what it was all about, but I knew he had a good business and was considered a wealthy man," Fred relates. "He explained that he had taken notice of me when I handled the insurance end with DeRose, and that I had impressed him favorably. He said he was a bachelor, had no family, and since his health had taken a turn for the worse (heart trouble), he wanted me to work for him in his business, and that when I had mastered it, he would leave the company in my hands entirely and retire to California. His operation, I felt, was good for $50,000 a year — so that the whole deal seemed like one of those Horatio Alger story books. After a rather long discussion with my wife, she also felt this was a great opportunity that could not be overlooked, even though it meant the bookstore idea would have to be shelved.

"I went with Fred Forrester in August of 1927, and he was like a father to me — and also to Frances. Many people thought 'Old Man Forrester' (as we called him) was brusque, rather biting in his manner. I felt he was a man of culture, and he showered good deeds on me. He would frequently take us to dinner at the Brown Palace, to operas and the theatre, and seemingly couldn't do enough for us. We were among the few people he ever invited to his house, which he shared with a big dog called Shep who, by the way, was pretty jealous of his master.

"In the meantime I was learning the business, and in a few months I knew all the 'angles,' so to speak. I started soliciting new accounts, and he complimented me on this. He had been in business for years, but did not show very many Jewish accounts on his books. He would say, 'Why don't you go see some of your Jewish friends and bring back some business from them?' I actually didn't know anyone at the business establishments he told me to solicit, like the May Company, or Shwayder's.

However, I went out and I did get some new clients. I also managed to write insurance with other firms — non-Jewish — that he had never been able to crack, like the American National Bank. I talked to one of the vice presidents, Mr. Hotaling, and told him I knew a lot of Italian-Americans in Denver whom I might be able to convince to open accounts at his bank, and that got the business for me."

This was an enjoyable period in Fred's life, but it came to a sudden and unexpected end. One day in November a call came to Forrester advising him that one of the buildings he had insured was on fire. He left the office to investigate and did not show up at the office the next day. "I wasn't too concerned the first day, but when he didn't show up the day after, I went to his house. Even before I went in I could hear Shep barking. Anyway, I found him in bed, where he had died of a heart attack.

"I felt suddenly adrift, and the high hopes I had built up for a successful insurance business were squashed. Forrester had left an old will, dated about ten years earlier, which bequeathed everything — his business, his real estate, his stocks — to the Society for the Prevention of Cruelty to Animals. The Colorado National Bank was his executor, and since they did not have anyone in the Trust Department who knew as much about his business as I did, they asked me to administer the Forrester estate, advising me that I could have an office in the Bank until the estate was settled.

"When I had completed my project at the bank, sometime in January or February of 1928, the road became wide open for the realization of my longtime desire to start a bookstore." It was to be six months before circumstances were right for the germination of the new venture, and meanwhile Frances continued working and Fred sold some insurance on his own, intermingled with the buying and selling of a few books.

By June Fred felt he should take another trip East, gathering more material for the new store-to-be. Actually, the trip probably wasn't necessary, but Fred felt that the enterprise would be more interesting to Frances if she were to accompany him on a book-buying tour. It was, in essence, a second honeymoon, and an opportunity for his wife to meet his grandmother, aunts, uncles, and cousins still living in Rochester, and for him to meet some of Frances's relatives in Boston. In the month-long tour they followed the normal circle route Fred had developed over the years, visiting Kansas City, St. Louis, Cincinnati, Washington, Baltimore, Philadelphia, New York City, Boston, then to a family reunion at Rochester, a purely social visit to Niagara Falls and Toronto, then to Buffalo, Cleveland, Chicago and, finally, Denver.

The trip achieved its purpose. Frances could participate in a much more personal way in corresponding with Fred's business associates as well as his family and friends. She would remember with affection the bookmen, such as William C. Smith of Cincinnati; the Jolsons in Washington; the Italian dinner with the Bennetts; and the delightful Alfred Goldsmith, his round cherubic face smiling as he related to Frances the story of Fred bringing the mint copy of Walt Whitman's *Leaves of Grass* to his bookstore in New York City.

When they returned, it was with renewed excitement and enthusiasm for Project Bookstore. "I had started actively hunting for a suitable location," Fred recalls, his eyes still sparkling at the memory, "when the three stores operated by the Adair family became available as a result of an involuntary bankruptcy. The Government Referee sold off all the assets at retail to the public. But I had my eye on one of the locations — 406 Fifteenth Street at Tremont [at that time, the "new" part of downtown and eventually to be across the street from the May Company–Denver Hilton complex, but then known as Courthouse Square] — which I thought was attractive, not only because of the low rent but also because it had housed a book business for more than ten years. It had been The Old Colony Bookstore before Adair had taken it over.

"The Government finally sold off everything except for the bare, dilapidated shelving, a safe and a few racks, and I paid their modest asking price for the shell that was left. Then I signed a lease with the estate which owned the building, and we were in business!"

With Fred's background, his collection of rare books and expensive first editions, most of the existing bookstores in Denver at the time may have assumed he would specialize in the old and rare and perhaps call his operation something like "The Western Americana Book Shop" or another non-flamboyant, low-key designation. But Fred was more than a dealer in rare books — his experience with the Denver Book Shop taught him the value of merchandising, of appealing to the man-on-the-street.

"I chose the name 'Bargain Book Store' in order to head the alphabetical list of bookstores in the phone directory, and because I thought it was a good name. And it turned out later to be a fine choice, since it appealed to students who bought secondhand textbooks, a phase of the book business we ended up with inadvertently. We took over the store on the twentieth of November, 1928, but the government had paid the rent until December 1, so we were there at the benefit of the government for over a week.

"I hurriedly began to move the books in from my parents' house and in two or three days had a respectable miscellaneous stock on the shelves. During the course of these energetic activities I somehow 'forgot' to remove the Government's bankruptcy and close-out sale signs which were plastered all over the windows, and I'm sure that some people were under the impression the Government was still running the sale, which didn't hurt the business any. I did pull off all the signs on the first of the month, but we had an excellent first week. And our hopes were high for the future."

The year of 1929 started with great optimism, not only for the Rosenstocks but for the country in general. Economists of the day were bullish on America, either ignoring or unaware of the subtle indications that the boom would become the bust before the year had run its course. Fortunately for Fred and Frances they had the time to become established. "First and limited editions of books were fetching good prices," Fred recalls, "and the rare book business was booming."

And then came along another of the so-called "miracles" which would prove so important to the success of the business during the depression years. "When the government sold off the books from Adair's bankruptcy sale, there was a lot of stuff in the basement that nobody wanted: about one hundred fifty packages of books with labels like *Glory to God,* and *Jesus and I,* on the outside. They were Catholic schoolbooks.

"The Adairs had had a corner on the Catholic schoolbook business — and also a good share of the public school business. In those days, high school pupils had to buy their own books. Came the first part of September and the kids started streaming in to buy books, and I didn't think I had any of the texts they needed! Then I remembered some of the titles and rushed downstairs to the basement to empty out the books from the packages for the Catholic students. I sold something like $1,200 worth in an hour! Before they left I had obtained the names of the principals of their schools. And I asked them to make a list of the books they needed so I could place an order for them. The orders went to the publishers by telegram, and in one week I was in the Catholic schoolbook business. Before long selling schoolbooks was really our bread and butter."

Fred Rosenstock's flair for merchandising was not something that was calculated. He had an inherent desire to please people, whether they were real estate prospects, insurance clients, collectors of rare books, or a kid with a list of schoolbook titles clutched in a dirty fist.

"We began to advertise 'Sound, Sanitary, Secondhand Schoolbooks,' and we meant it. We had a special method of cleaning books. I hate to use the word 'invented,' but nobody else had done it. We had a shaver that would pare off the old worn edges of the books, making them look like new — or at least clean. Then we began to repair breaks, training girls to do this work. We used a binder's glue which was flexible but at the same time would hold the repaired places together. We would examine a book for missing pages, and from a special section of defective copies would pull out pages to replace those that were missing.

"I began to contact wholesale companies specializing in schoolbooks, and including them in my itinerary on my book-buying trips to the East.

I arranged to acquire books from twenty or twenty-five wholesalers, and as a result would have secondhand books that my customers weren't able to get anywhere else in Denver. I used my connections to obtain the red anniversary edition of *Gregg Shorthand,* 300 copies in one lot — a real coup, schoolbookwise. Because of things like this, we captured the schoolbook business in Denver. And Frances was a very prominent part of all this, more active than I was in that part of our operation.

"Although I would do the hiring, she was in charge of the girls who did the repairing and cleaning. At times we had twenty to twenty-five people working in the store. It wasn't unusual for kids to line up for a block trying to get their books for the new semester. We didn't have any computers in those days, and everybody was treated as an individual — actually, everybody was a friend. We ran the business in the old country style, and that was the way we enjoyed it."

That was the beginning, the transformation of the Fred Rosenstock dream into a reality. His enthusiasm was unbounded — but he, along with millions of other Americans, did not know that the economy was on a precipice of disaster. In September of 1929 he was enjoying the flush of success, and was making his plans for an extensive trip East in October.

CHAPTER VIII

AN EASTERN ADVENTURE

THE SCHOOLBOOK RUSH HAD ENDED, and Fred was eager to travel east. "Seek and ye shall find" was his motto, and one of the great enjoyments of his life was rummaging through bookstores searching for that elusive vein of gold.

Preparations were extensive, deciding which books he would take, what catalogs and pamphlets would be most helpful. "They were mainly literary; in other words, first editions, early printed books, press books — not western history. This was before the stock market crash of 1929," he notes, "a period when first editions, both English and American, were bringing the top prices. Things were riding high. Collectors were plentiful; items were hard to get and in demand. Publishers were putting out even new books in both limited and regular editions, and there was such a demand for the limited, autographed editions in those days that if you didn't order in advance you wouldn't get the item. There has never since been the demand for first editions as there was at that time.

"I would usually start out with anywhere from twenty-five to fifty or sixty rare items. The idea would be to sell these books to the rare book dealers in New York, the specialists in first editions. Along the way I would pick up other books, which I would sell sometimes the next day. But the books I brought from Denver I would sell to stores like Scribner's, the Bennett Book Studios (which dealt in fine first editions), and G. A. Baker and Company, an excellent firm whose owner was one of the great bookmen of all time — his name was Harzof.

"At that time, outside of ten or twelve book dealers in the United States, the bookstores across the country were really not up on their trade. They didn't know much. As a matter of fact, there was little information available for reference. There were no price tags in those days. You would have to be alert yourself, keep up with the auction records, and make a special study of the whole trade.

"I was interested in English first editions, but frankly that whole end of the business was too complicated. But I did know American first editions, and these were in the greatest demand of all. Not only the old and great authors such as Thoreau, Whitman, Emerson, Longfellow, but lesser names as well. It was only the high spots of the famous authors that the collectors were looking for. For instance, out of forty or fifty books that Longfellow wrote, only four or five were of real value. Collectors were looking for first editions of *Hyperion, Evangeline,* or *Voices in the Night.* Cooper wrote perhaps forty novels, but the search was for first editions of *The Spy* or *The Last of the Mohicans,* and possibly one or two others. With Thoreau, who wrote at least a dozen books, the demand was for only two of them (and one or two posthumous items published long after his death in very limited editions), the first edition of *Walden* with its respective first edition points, and *Week on the Concord and Merrimac.*

"About that time there was a revival in the demand for the first editions of Emily Dickinson. All of a sudden there was a big splurge and search for Emily Dickinson first editions. I probably cleared the country of all the available first editions of Dickinson. I made up my mind that I was going to hunt for Dickinson, and I believe I found just about all the first edition copies that were available on dealers' shelves.

"In those days I was probably one of the few bookmen who made it a point to travel across the country to both buy and sell. To come from a distance like I did all the way to New York, riding by train, was quite a novel thing for a bookseller, then from New York to Goodspeeds and other stores in Boston.

"In Kansas City I stopped at Kramers and the Kansas City Book

Exchange, two stores that were really treasure houses. Neither of them made a pretense of checking or learning about first editions. They knew the authors, but they didn't know the points and they didn't care too much. We were always good friends, and they didn't mind if I picked up an expensive item for practically nothing. 'Oh, Mr. Rosenstock,' they would greet me, 'you're here again. What have you bought recently?' They would even call me into their private offices and show me books that were still unmarked and unopened.

"Those stores in Kansas City were general bookstores. I was mainly looking for fine literature in first editions, beautifully printed and beautifully bound books, but I would also find saleable schoolbooks in these stores. I was also beginning to buy Western Americana, not with any intention of becoming an expert like I did later, but, for example, if I were to find an interesting book dealing with Fremont I'd buy it on general principles.

"In St. Louis I would always go to Miner's. This was a fine store, and William Harvey Miner was a great man in the book business. There were no steals, so to speak, in Miner's shop, but it was a distinction to be able to go to Miner's and be received by him in a friendly manner, have him show you what he had. He was a very fine person, and I felt that William Harvey Miner was one of the men I respected most and considered it a special pleasure to know.

"I usually saw C. B. Finley in St. Louis. Finley was not a bookseller, but a book scout. In those days I used to advertise for special items, and although he didn't have a shop and actually worked in a haberdashery during the day, he was quite an intelligent bookman. He visited the antique shops and rummage sales where he would pick up some nice books which he would save for me or, if particularly important, would write to me — just because we had become good friends."

In Cincinnati, Fred visited two bookstores, the Traveller's Book Shop and Smith's Book Store. Traveller's was a general bookstore, with some fine sets, but a limited collectors' section. Smith's, however, was a high point of his trip. The owner, William C. Smith, "was the greatest bookman in the business." Actually, at the time Fred knew him, he no longer had a retail store, concentrating as a collector. His specialty was rare books on southern history and general Americana. In his search for particular items he would occasionally have to buy complete libraries, with volumes that he did not wish to list in his catalog. Many of these he would hold until Fred Rosenstock made one of his periodic visits.

"Smith was on the eighth floor of the Union Central Life Insurance building, right in the heart of the downtown area. Those were prohibition days, but the first thing Smith would say was, 'Hi, Fred, how about a drink?' He'd even ask you what brand you wanted, whether you wanted scotch or bourbon or a cordial. Each bottle was behind a particular book or set of books. So, if you wanted Old Crow, he knew exactly where it was. I was never really a drinking man, but with Smith you had to start out with a drink.

"The first time I went to his office the biggest surprise was that there were no rows of shelves filled with books — just a few behind his desk, and you had the feeling they were there just to hide the whiskey. Anyway, once in his office, I'd sit beside his desk and he'd say, 'Well, look over my cards.' There were two or three card files and I'd start to go through them. He had a secretary who would take the cards I'd selected and she would go to the back room, find the books and bring them out. I'd probably find twenty or thirty books in the card file and we'd sit and talk while she was getting the actual books.

"He always gave me a special discount on everything. It would take me quite a while to check the books and make my selection. I sometimes had to force myself to remember that I wasn't running a store just for collectors, but for the general public, so I'd have to make buys that would have a broader appeal. After I'd seen the catalogued items, I'd say, 'Well, now, Bill, let me see some of those books that you are *forced* to buy.' He didn't have them on shelves, but in cartons. Not organized and not too convenient to look at. Some of the books he had dumped into the cartons were beautiful items, but he just wasn't interested in them and had been holding them, waiting for me to come. Many of them were wonderful books for my general stock and I was glad to get them.

"Bill Smith helped me greatly. He could have sold those books to others, to stores in New York or Boston, but he liked me. I was his friend, and he was somebody special to me. He died in the early 1970s at the age of ninety-three.

"In Washington, D.C., Lowdermilk's was the outstanding dealer in history-related books, and perhaps the oldest. At that time, they'd been in business seventy-five or eighty years. They were especially strong in out-of-print government publications in every field — geology, anthropology, archaeology. You could find in their storeroom reports and documents published way back in the 1810s, 1820s, 1830s. Some were in the original envelopes that the government intended to mail them in. Lowdermilk bought remainders from the U.S. Printing Office.

"You could find the original reports of Fremont, Powell, the surveys of the Colorado River, and the thirteen-volume set of the surveys the government issued in the 1850s with a view to establishing a cross-country railroad. They had hired the best surveyors and the greatest artists of that day to plan the route and to sketch and make paintings of the scenery. It's titled *Explorations and Surveys for a Railroad Route from the Mississippi River to the Pacific Ocean.* And there were great artists involved, like John Mix Stanley, Eastman, Müllhausen, and others.

"Lowdermilk's continued in business until the late sixties — it was one of the last great general bookstores in the United States.

"I also used to call on Whyte's in Washington. They didn't deal in modern first editions at all, but had a fine collection of books printed in the 1400s, 1500s, 1600s, 1700s. Whyte's specialized in books like Dryden's poems, Boswell's *Life of Johnson,* Hakluyt's *Voyages,* Beaumont and Fletcher, Shakespeare, all of them in contemporary bindings. I can't recall another store like this in the United States at that time: nothing but books of this type in old English bindings, and all in fine condition. This man was such a fastidious book lover himself, besides being a businessman, that every month or so he would take one section of his stock and go over every book with a special preparation to keep the bindings soft. And then he would apply some kind of polish to make them appear almost like new — in an old sort of way. To me, this was another treasure trove, and I bought many, many fine books from him, naturally in the field of English literature.

"One call I always enjoyed in Washington was to Luther Cornwall, a big, gruff, fat man who had been in the book business for many years. His was a general book business, but he had a special interest in geology, and I was particularly interested in his out-of-print geological publications that the government had sponsored.

"His was a general antiquarian book store, and although he had an assorted stock, it was well-organized and you didn't have to wade through thousands of books in order to find what you were looking for. This was unusual for those days. Usually secondhand bookstores were places where the bookmen didn't know what they had. Everything was scattered, and the stock was not only on the shelves but in piles on the floor. I tended to find more in Cornwall's than in Lowdermilk's, and I always thought of Luther Cornwall as being of the more intelligent, knowledgeable booksellers of his time.

"I'd also visit the 'Big Book Shop,' which was just a fast merchandise mart. They bought and sold fiction and remainders. It was called, in old bookseller's vernacular, 'a schlock store.' In other words, they bought books by the yard and sold them by the yard. Occasionally I'd find some schoolbooks there.

"When I left Washington, I would go by train to Baltimore and Philadelphia. Those old smoky trains, with the foul air and the soot coming through the windows . . . But I would spend my time thinking of what I had just bought on my last stop, and I didn't mind the soot at all.

"The Peabody Book Shop in Baltimore was owned by two bright young Jewish brothers. They did carry new books, but they specialized in what you would call *avante garde* literature — books by D. H. Law-

rence, poetry by Edna St. Vincent Millay. In addition to that, they specialized in modern — not early — American first editions.

"On my 1929 trip I bought two O. Henry first editions from them.
At that time, O. Henry was a 'modern' author. In those days he was
avidly collected, but today you can't give an O. Henry first edition away.

"I would also stop at Smith's Book Store in Baltimore, a general
bookstore, similar to those in Kansas City. These were the kinds of
stores I would look over very carefully, knowing that once in a while I
might find a rare book in a stack on the floor.

"Two dealers in Philadelphia I would call on were Young and Williams, both a bit peculiar — or let's say, unusual. Jim Williams was a
book dealer who formerly had a shop in Colorado Springs. A very
smart, energetic bookseller, he was also a marvelous scout. But he had a
very bad case of TB, and there were long periods when he couldn't work
or would be hospitalized. After he left the Springs, he opened a store in
Philadelphia and got married. I would stay at their home, and once he
offered to drive me to New York in his Model A Ford. 'I'm going to
New York anyway,' he said, 'but I have a few stops to make in New
Jersey.' We went through some places I'd never seen before, like Princeton, and Camden — Walt Whitman's town. It took about two days to
get to New York, with all the places we had to stop. In Elizabeth, there
was a dealer by the name of Noah Morrison, and he called his bookshop
'Noah's Ark' and had built it in the shape of an ark.

"Williams was an inveterate gambler and he insisted that I play a
game called single-handed poker. It could be murderous. Sometimes, in
order to buy good books I had to play poker with him, since the stakes
were that if I should win he would have to sell to me. And that's how I
used to do business with Williams.

"The other man in Philadelphia was Nat Young. He was very intelligent, had a Master's Degree from Temple University, and taught English literature for awhile. The unusual thing about Young was that he
had acquired his knowledge of literature in college — when most of the
collectors and book dealers learned through experience.

"For obvious reasons, New York City was the climax of my eastern trips. Alfred Goldsmith had a little shop there, and I used to have my mail forwarded to his place. Like so many places along Lexington Avenue — where he was located — you had to go down three steps from the ground level. His letterhead had a picture of a sparrow on it, and his store was called 'At the Sign of the Sparrow.'

"On Fourth Avenue at that time there must have been thirty booksellers in a stretch of three blocks. One dealer, Ben Harris, had a stock of mostly junk on his shelves. But if you got to know him, as I did, he would trot out some very choice things from the back room. These special items he'd never put on the shelves, but would offer them to big dealers like Scribner's, or to a few special collectors. If you didn't know, and you walked in and this big fat fellow dressed in an open shirt and no tie was sitting behind his old desk, you would probably leave thinking that his place was the worst junk shop in New York."

Fred spent a considerable amount of time in New York, for it was here that he did most of his selling, and considerable buying. His experience at New York auctions, whether buying or selling, didn't appear to be in Fred's favor. "I usually would enter an auction house before an auction without any special plans to buy a particular book, but just out of curiosity I would go in and look. There is something about the electrification and the enthusiasm that infects you, and almost without realizing it or knowing what you're doing, you find yourself in a scramble for an item trying to overbid somebody. The minute you get the item, you feel you've overpaid, and at the end you usually walk out wishing you had never come in."

Boston and Goodspeed's was the next stop. "Goodspeed's was as fine a store in 1929 as it is in 1976. George E. Goodspeed, Jr., who founded the business, wrote a book of reminiscences before he died — in the late twenties, when he was approaching eighty. His son, George III, was running the business when I was there, and was about thirty — around my age. He's still running it in 1976. Not only did they publish fine catalogs, done with knowledge, scholarship, and good, fair judgment of values, but they also put out a monthly magazine for collectors. It was called *The Month* and was very informative about good books."

In a letter to Frances, Fred writes, "I bought some very good stuff but it cost me real money. First I bought from Goodspeed's one of the very rarest of Whitman items, next to the first edition of 1855 by far the best Whitman. It is *Leaves of Grass Imprints,* 1860. The item was a small pamphlet, not actually written by Whitman. It's mostly criticisms by other editors and reviewers of Whitman's *Leaves of Grass*. It was put out by a Boston publisher, and was sort of a consensus of criticisms. It was a very, very rare item, but in a Whitman collection, it's an absolute must. Whitman had to make a public defense of himself after being criticized very hotly.

"I paid $315 for it at that time. Strangely enough, it hasn't increased too much in value — it's probably worth at most $500 to $600 today.

"I also visited a store in Boston called Smith and McCance — a fine establishment but not nearly the store that Goodspeed's was. They dealt in general secondhand books and actually I found more here than at Goodspeed's. Possibly because they didn't know their business as well. I hate to put it that bluntly, but they weren't specialists and they didn't segregate their select items — so you could find an exceptional volume right on the shelves with their ordinary books."

That was the easternmost point on the circle trip and once again bookbuyer Rosenstock was traveling west. With Frances in Denver and his bookstore flourishing, Fred was getting impatient to return home, while at the same time enjoying this phase of the business, one that kept him in contact with old friends: books and booksellers. Fortunately the record of his 1929 trip was made more complete since he was writing to Frances several times a week, and those letters were preserved.

He was en route to Buffalo, and passed through his home town of Rochester without stopping. "Rochester never had any serious interest for me in the way of bookstores, and Frances and I had visited all the relatives on our trip in 1928." His anxiety was obvious in a letter from Buffalo: "A week from tomorrow I'll be home with my honey."

"Ulrichs was the only halfway decent store in Buffalo. Toronto, my next stop, had some interesting bookstores. There was something like Fourth Avenue in New York, called Yonge Street. But the outstanding bookstore — still in business in 1975 — was called Albert Britnell and Son, and that is where I found some fine old English books. Britnell would import seventeenth and eighteenth century books, in fine bindings from England."

Fred passed through Cleveland and Detroit quickly. "Detroit and Cleveland still are almost devoid of fine bookshops. For some reason, those two — it might be because they have large factory-working populations — weren't interested in the type of thing I was dealing in then. They seemed to be more interested in current books and fiction, and I never went much for what we call ordinary books. There was one good store in Cleveland called Burrows Brothers. They had a general bookstore on the ground floor, but had the choice plums up on the balcony.

"Chicago was a center of the book business, second only to New York. One store was named Targ and Dordick, started by two young Jewish boys and specializing in first editions. They had a little hole-in-the-wall, no money; just two poor boys who were enthusiastic about books, particularly the modern, *avante garde* type. Targ, in later years, wrote some fine books on book collecting, one called *A Carousel for Book Collectors*. He also wrote several bibliographies, and became sales editor for the World Publishing Company in Cleveland. But I knew them when they started, and when I would buy a book from them for ten dollars I had the feeling they wanted to give me the store.

"Another of my very best friends in Chicago was Frank Rosengren, a great dealer, very forward thinking, acting, and intelligent. He was not Jewish, although his name sounds Jewish. 'Rosengreen' would be Jewish, but 'Rosengren' was Danish. Frank had health problems, and also had a son who suffered from asthma. He finally moved to San Antonio and started a bookstore there. Frank died in the later '40s, but his wife, Florence, still runs the finest bookstore in San Antonio.

"There were other bookmen in Chicago who were close friends, and who were excellent in their special fields. One was Wright Howes, *bibliophile extraordinaire*. When I first came to Chicago he ran a little shop specializing mainly in first editions, although in later years he became a recognized authority in points and values of historical Americana.

"Another was the unforgettable Ben Abramson — a distorted genius if there ever was, with a magnetic, charming personality, yet completely unpredictable. But he had a fine shop, specializing in modern literature and press books, with a tinge of erotica. He owned the Argus Book Shop, and also published a series of 'classics,' beautiful but somewhat gaudily designed, and illustrated by famous artists of the day. One artist, I recall, was Clara Tice.

"One of my closest friends among Chicago bookmen was Jerry Nedwick, always tremendously helpful on my visits, and not only in a business way. In 1928 when Frances and I went to Chicago on our belated honeymoon the Nedwicks, who were taking off on a vacation, insisted that we stay in their downtown apartment. A secondhand dealer, he was known in the business as a 'swashbuckler,' but underlying the veneer he was shrewd, and also totally dependable and honest."

Leaving Chicago, it was a non-stop journey back to Denver for Fred Rosenstock, anxious to relate his experiences and describe his purchases to Frances. Denver collectors anticipated his return, eager to see what he had brought back. "I usually satisfied them," Fred noted. "I would show them things that ordinarily wouldn't be found in a comparatively young city, with no long lines of families going back four or five generations like Cincinnati, for example. So from Cincinnati and other places in the East I would really bring back thrillers. While possibly these items wouldn't bring great profits in themselves, the advertising that this gave me was greatly responsible for my reputation. In this manner I built a very fine business — by taking these trips and not waiting in Denver for these books to come to me, like manna from the sky."

By the time Fred had returned, the stock market crash had become a reality and the economy was in a tailspin. "Wasn't it terrible," he reflected, "that I bought all this stuff, probably at high prices, just before the crash. It was more than just a crash of money. That was a crash that shook the nation, and it took the heart and the spirit out of first edition collectors. That was the acme period of first edition collecting and it never has come back. When some interest did return, it was with different authors, and never with the same vitality and national demand. I was riding high on the last two or three years of that first edition surge.

"For example, a first issue of the first edition of *Two Years Before the Mast* by Dana brought $1250 at that time. Forty years later it's not worth as much as it was then — I'd say not over $600. A first edition of Washington Irving's *Knickerbocker History of New York* sold for $1200 at the high point in 1929. Today you could pick up the same item for $300 or $400."

For Fred Rosenstock, it marked the end of a period. Although he continued collecting, as he always would, he no longer specialized in first editions, but turned his interest to Western Americana, not only in the accumulation of one of the finest collections of western history books assembled by a single individual, but broadening his scope to other forms of art, especially Charles Russell paintings and sculptures.

But this was the end of 1929, the beginning of the darkest economic era in America's history, and Fred Rosenstock may well have been praying for another Rosenstock "miracle."

CHAPTER IX

SURVIVAL YEARS

ON OCTOBER 29, 1929, blue chip stocks on the New York Stock Exchange dropped an average of $40 per share in value, marking the end of postwar prosperity. Before the end of that year, losses on the market would total $15 billion, and by the time the 1932 New Year's Eve had rolled around the figure would be in excess of $50 billion. Unemployment would reach the unfathomable number of twelve million.

The book business suffered along with industry in general, but most of the major publishers were able to survive. In 1929 the total number of books printed reached 235 million — by 1931 the figure was 154 million, and in 1933 dipped to an all-time low of 120 million. Fiction books suffered the most, and schoolbooks — Fred Rosenstock's specialty at this time — the least. Physical changes, however, were taking place in schoolbooks. Few textbooks in the twenties had any particular eye appeal, but by the thirties, partly due to competition, partly to increasing sophistication in the educational system, some of the major textbook publishers started hiring designers and art directors and schoolbooks took on a new, more attractive look.

Frances's brother, Nelson Goodman, a frequent assistant at the store in his pre-med years, recalls that early period. "The depression years were indeed difficult. An all-out effort was put forth to promote the sale of textbooks. Fred called on all the parochial schools personally and became acquainted with all the principals. He organized an advertising campaign whereby his cards and blotters were distributed at every major school in the city by the pupils, and the sales force at the store consisted of bright young students specially trained by Fred to handle the sale of textbooks.

"In addition to this, he felt that he must justify the name 'Bargain' and actually provided books at lower prices to students during this period. He made every effort to locate used books outside of Denver that he could obtain at lower prices. They were frequently soiled and marked up when they arrived, but all were cleaned and repaired before being offered for sale.

"With all the effort expended, business prospered making possible the acquisitions of Americana and Western art. The textbooks were still his primary source of income, but the emphasis began to shift gradually to the more interesting fields of publishing, especially Western history. As his reputation increased, more and more people would come into the store and engage him in conversation about their private collections."

Fred not only had a deep interest in the West, but a knack for drawing out of those who came into his store tidbits of information. He would talk to them about their pioneer relatives and would frequently discover that these acquaintances had old diaries, maps, pictures or books in their basements or attics. As Nelson Goodman remembers, "These conversations would not always bring immediate results, but years later some of these folks would have a change in circumstance and would offer their libraries for sale to Fred.

"Even though the schoolbook business took precedence over all else (at this time), and Americana and book publishing were occupying his thoughts, he realized that there was an increasing demand for technical books and geological publications. He soon acquired one of the most complete stocks of these items in the Rocky Mountain region. As his reputation grew, so his opportunities to purchase private libraries from geologists and teachers increased."

Life in the somewhat remote, mile-high city of Denver during the thirties and early forties was relaxed and leisurely, and the Bargain Book Store became a warm and friendly haven for students, teachers, collectors, and authors, as well as bookish characters seeking refuge and conversation. Many came to buy, of course, or to sell, but others shuffled in to talk, to trade, to borrow money, to while away an hour or so. Whatever the reason for their visit, they were never turned away. Frequently, if it appeared to Fred that his companions were in need, he would terminate the conversation with a suggestion: "Let's go across the street and I'll buy you a meal."

Throughout the depression, Fred remained steadfast in practicing what he considered a formula for success. He never took a customer for granted, but trained every employee to treat whomever was in the store as a valued friend; advertise truthfully, but advertise; and never underestimate the importance of public relations. Not only did he pass out leaflets and notebooks and blotters at the schools, but he advertised his sales in the local newspapers and eventually developed a radio program. William E. Walsh, a member of the faculty at Regis college in Denver, wrote the script for a series of studies called "Portraits in Literature," presented over one of the major radio stations every Sunday evening, and sponsored by Fred Rosenstock, proprietor of The Bargain Book Store.

Merchandising and public relations during the depression years required extraordinary effort as well as ingenuity. School district budgets were cut drastically, particularly in the area of book purchasing. In the 1930s, Harold S. Lindbloom, a book salesman for Scott, Foresman and Company, was transferred from the Northwest to Colorado, Wyoming, and Utah. "I found one of my leading accounts, apart from school districts, was the Bargain Book Store in Denver, Fred and Frances Rosenstock, proprietors. The depression had put something of a crimp in the pupil-purchase of textbooks, but the Rosenstocks, as retailers of textbooks, did not give up easily. They kept the dealer's plight squarely before school administration officials and Fred often represented the Denver textbook dealers as a group. Incidentally and ironically, one of the dealers he represented was William Dietrich, head of the Communist party in Colorado for several years and a one-time no-chance candidate for governor. At that time he owned the Auditorium Bookstore.

The Bargain Book Store

Window display at the Bargain Book Store

"The Rosenstocks," Lindbloom recalls, "kept going on minimal profits and maximal service and coordination in their handling of textbooks, going after not only what little remained of 'pupil-purchase' in the public schools, but small school elementary orders, Catholic and other parochial orders, even college and university orders." Harold Lindbloom would eventually become a partner of Fred Rosenstock's in the schoolbook publishing business.

In an effort to provide books at a minimum cost during these difficult years, Fred proposed a plan to Denver schoolbook dealers, pooling orders so that carload shipments could be made. He acted as coordinator between the Chicago suppliers, the dealers, and the teachers and school administrators.

Another Rosenstock innovation developed in the thirties was the forerunner of today's "bookmobile." To make it easier for the outlying public libraries in Colorado towns such as Boulder, Greeley, Fort Collins, or Sterling, Fred decided to "take the bookstore to the library," loading up a passenger car with selected titles and touring the northeast part of the state. Nelson Goodman did the driving (Fred never learned to drive a car!), and Fred would do the selling, inviting librarians to examine the books in his car. These were secondhand books, and with book budgets at an all-time low, libraries were pleased to be able to acquire exceptional titles at bargain prices. Eventually, he became so knowledgeable about the interests and needs of different libraries that he would gather up a selection and spread them out on the library steps, knowing he would sell a good percentage.

While still with DeRose, Fred had started selling fireworks, a profitable sideline he continued until the end of the depression era. Although it had a short season, the fireworks business expanded until there were Rosenstock fireworks stores in strategic locations all over Denver. A sister of Frances, Edith Permut, was one of the dozens of employees who participated. "The biggest incentive in getting us to work was not the salary but the promise of taking home the fireworks that were not sold."

"The evening of the Fourth," Fred notes, "when the sale was over, I would stage a fireworks display that would rival the best in the city. After all, there was no point in keeping an inventory, and I couldn't think of a more colorful way to dispose of it."

While the Rosenstocks were using a combination of hard work and imagination to survive, the rate of business failures throughout the country was appalling. "In 1932," Fred relates, "I wrote a letter to a customer, Dr. Arthur Vos of Cincinnati, which had a note of despondency in it. His response is an interesting reflection of the conditions that were prevalent at the time: 'When I read your letter yesterday I gave it a good deal of thought, because I realized that my small orders were helping you out. I trust and hope, my good friend, that you will be able to weather the terrible depression successfully. Under the present conditions of affairs, I will do my best to give you an order now and then; so cheer up if you can.' "

"In Cincinnati," he wrote, "many of the big businesses have been shot to hell. The conditions here are terrible. Crain and Hawley, the largest plumbing manufacturers and suppliers, had to be closed. Procter and Gamble has laid off hundreds of men and the report is current that they are on the rocks. The Blondel Milling Machine Company, and Mr. Blondel (the head of it), a million-dollar man, have lost all they had. He played the stock market and lost every dollar.

"I want you to know I reconnoitered the various book stores in Cincinnati and I have been greatly disappointed in them. What impressed me greatly was the absence of sets of books, and most of these stores were shabby and shoddy looking. When I think of your store with the many new books and fine sets which encourages sales, I wonder how these bookstores in Cincinnati make a living."

Dr. Vos, assuredly facing his own problems, was concerned about Fred Rosenstock. As Fred philosophized, "Our customers were our friends, and they really wanted us to survive."

And survival was dependent upon the schoolbook business, although his heart was in Western Americana. In an exchange of letters with Whitman Bennett in 1932 Fred wrote that "there is little demand in

Colorado for first editions, and that schoolbooks — the most uninterest-ing part of the business — has been responsible for keeping it alive. As you probably know, I have been confining more and more attention to Western Americana, and I expect to issue a catalog purely of this class of material in the very near future." A year before, in 1931, he had issued his first catalog, a general listing including only 465 items. It was 1934 before a second Rosenstock catalog of Western Americana finally appeared.

From the modest profits during those difficult years, more and more money was channeled toward the collecting of books, manuscripts, arti-facts, and paintings relating to the West. Extensive trips to the East could no longer be justified, but he continued to travel by car, with Nelson Goodman at the wheel, to various parts of Colorado and the midwest.

To be successful in the book business, it was essential to be a shrewd merchandiser when selling, but it was equally important to be a shrewd buyer. And Fred Rosenstock was — and still is — a master at both. In his words, "When browsing through a secondhand store, you might ask, 'Do you have any books on Lewis and Clark?' not mentioning a specific title, because just asking was enough to make the price go up." If he were to locate a particularly rare item, he would frequently select three or four unimportant volumes as well, sandwiching the prize in the mid-dle. "It was best to take it to a clerk who was pretty busy, or didn't seem particularly up on Western material. I was willing to pay the price they were asking, but I didn't want to pay a premium because I showed too much interest in it."

One of the reasons why Fred became known as "the rarest of the rare" was his skill in developing contacts, such as his establishing a rela-tionship with William Jackson Books Limited, export booksellers in London, England. He selected a group of English authors who were still producing at that time — Aldous Huxley, D. H. Lawrence, H. M. Tomlinson, Somerset Maugham, John Galsworthy, and others — and gave Jackson a standing order to send five copies of each new title by any

Fred and Frances in the Bargain Book Store

of these authors as soon as it appeared. No other dealer in Denver had such a fine collection of English first editions by these noted authors, and Fred's reputation in this area continued to grow.

Standing orders were also placed through Jackson for books published by the fine English presses, such as Ashendene, Doves Press, Fanfrolico, Golden Cockerel, and the Vale Press. Children's classics illustrated by Arthur Rackham and Edmund Dulac of England were acquired as soon as they were published, as well as volumes illustrated by American artists Howard Pyle and N. C. Wyeth.

By the early thirties, Fred was receiving offers to buy collections and private libraries, but not in as great a quantity as he anticipated, considering the need people had for money at that time. As he wrote to Whitman Bennett, "One thing is remarkable to me during this depression — the lack of fine collections (either first editions or Americana) that are coming into the market, auction or otherwise. Even here in Denver it is an event when one of our dealers picks up even a 'half-way' decent lot. The universal idea seems to be to hold on to things of value, and *not* sell anything unless simply *forced* to do so."

Businesses have various milestones, different measuring sticks of success. To an advertising agency, it may be landing its first million-dollar account; to an insurance agent it's selling the million-dollar policy; to a publisher it's the first best-seller. To the rare book dealer, it is a mark of achievement when he issues his first catalog, baring to his peers the heart and soul of his collection.

In 1931 Fred Rosenstock defied the economic doomsayers and proceeded to publish a catalog entitled: *"Americana.* Colorado, Indians, Overland Expeditions, Texas, the Far West, etc., etc.; with the addition of a fine collection of books on Lincoln, the Civil War, and general American History." And the line at the bottom of the cover page read, "For Sale by Fred A. Rosenstock, 406 15th Street, Denver, Colorado."

It was not particularly impressive, including less than five hundred items, and although the catalog listed a number of rare items of interest to collectors, other dealers in the country were not visibly concerned about the first Rosenstock offering. It is significant as a hallmark in Fred's career, and as an item of memorabilia that provides some insight into the changes in values that have occurred in the thirty-five years since the catalog was issued.

The most expensive item listed was in the field of natural history, the folio edition of John James Audubon's *The Viviparous Quadrupeds of North America,* 1845–46–48, not only a significant book but far more beautiful and interesting than its unimaginative title would suggest. The original subscription price of this three-volume set was $300. "While this work will not approach the value of the great folio edition of Audubon's *Birds,*" the catalog states, "it is, nevertheless, a set that is due for a great advance in price." It was listed in the catalog for $500. In the Rosenstock Natural History catalog issued in 1941, he still had a set for $500. In 1964 a similar set sold at auction for $1,275, and in 1974 Fred Rosenstock would ask $15,000 for the first edition set in good condition.

Western Americana material has increased substantially in value over the past four decades, but ironically straight cowboy books — notwithstanding exposure on television — have not apreciated comparably. Charles Siringo's *Lone Star Cowboy* was listed in the Rosenstock catalog for $5.00, and in 1974 the dealer's price had increased only twenty dollars; *The Life of Tom Horn* showed a similar apreciation.

Robert E. Cowan, noted western bibliographer, wrote in 1931 that "Western Americana has at no time been plentiful. Printing in the primitive settlements was accomplished under unfavorable conditions and amidst unusual difficulties. Due to lack of material, editions were necessarily small. The destructive agencies of fire and flood frequently involved the printing offices along with many other buildings. The unsettled state of society and the nomadic habits of its population were not conducive to the collection or preservation of books. Finally, there has always been the unhappy success of the ignorantly disposed who each year ruthlessly destroy valuable material because they have never learned that perchance the trash of yesterday may become the treasure of tomorrow."

In 1920 the Arthur H. Clark Company catalog prefaced its list of books with an observation on "The Rapidly Increasing Scarcity of Americana: It is well known to the older and larger collectors that nearly all Americana, that is, books relating to this country, down to the past ten or twenty years, have been gathered from the many private collections in Great Britain . . . that source of supply is all but exhausted . . . there being no other country which has accumulated books relating to the United States . . . many of these books are going to be unobtainable. . . ."

Dr. A. S. W. Rosenbach, the dean of collectors, recalled (in 1927) that "when I first started to collect Americana it did not enjoy its present vogue. In the early days, you could buy amazingly important historical papers for a mere song." Few people had the foresight of Uncle Moses Pollock who had exclaimed to Dr. Rosenbach before the turn of the century: "My boy, Americana! That's the stuff to collect! Heaps of people can't seem to get it into their heads that there is just as much drama in the history of our own country as in any of the old world empires."

In his autobiographical volume, *Books and Bidders,* Dr. Rosenbach referred to a slim work entitled (or referred to as) the *Leonard Narrative:* "What would Zenas Leonard have thought had he known that his simple little narrative, published at Clearfield, Pennsylvania, in 1839, would in less than ninety years be battled for in the auction rooms? This tale of his adventures of five years' trapping for furs and trading with Indians in the Rocky Mountains is sought today as a most desirable addition to a library of Americana . . . I saw a copy sell at auction not long ago for $1700." This was written in 1927. Even Dr. Rosenbach might be surprised at this postscript: Fred Rosenstock placed a value on the *Leonard Narrative* of $8,500 in 1974, and suggested that it might well bring $12,000 at auction in the next few years.

Fortunately for the American heritage, collectors such as Dr. Rosenbach and Fred Rosenstock were on the scene to salvage from attics and basements many of these rare and irreplaceable records of the life and

history of this flamboyant, upstart country. And only a few such collectors existed in the twenties and early thirties. A survey, "Private Book
Collectors in the United States and Canada," published by R. R. Bowker
Company, revealed that only one out of ten collectors were located in
the West during the 1920s.

From his early days at the Denver Book Shop, Fred Rosenstock
maintained a mailing list of his customers interested in Americana. By
continuing contact with these collectors, Fred would learn what families
had important libraries, when and where the families moved, when a
collector died. In the latter case, he would let the heirs know that he was
available to help them dispose of their library at a fair price.

Through such contacts, as well as his extensive travels and acquaintance with book dealers throughout the country, Fred acquired more and
more items of general Americana, but with a gradual shift toward Western Americana, such as literary and historical accounts of the frontier,
the Indian, western exploration and travel. An almost paradoxical paral-
lel existed between the westward movement of the interests of readers
from the 1920s to the present, and the westward migration of the
American people in the nineteenth century.

Fred traces his own interest in the West to his days as a youth in
Rochester, when he had picked up some items of Americana in a secondhand bookstore and had sold them for a considerable profit to local
libraries.

"Because of my interest in books, my father arranged for me to be
the librarian in the reading room sponsored by the *Arbeiter Ring,* or
Workman's Circle, the Jewish local of the union for the clothing industry. I was only a boy, but it was here that I became acquainted with the
novels of Mayne Reid and other books about the West that had been
translated from English into Yiddish. So I read my first 'western' novels
in Yiddish."

The trend toward Western Americana had been firmly established
as the Rosenstock dream by the early thirties, and with the issuance of
his first "Western Americana" catalog in 1931 the die was cast.

Involved as he was in the schoolbook business as a prerequisite to survival, and devoting a substantial portion of his time to advertising campaigns, public relations, and correspondence with collectors and dealers throughout the country, it was not unusual, his sister-in-law Edith Permut recalls, "for him to be frequently pounding the keys of his typewriter at two or three o'clock in the morning. If he became tired, he would sleep on the counter for an hour or two — then get up and work again."

The nation was still immersed in economic chaos, but Fred Rosenstock had survived the labor pains of birth of the bookstore, and his future had all the promise of a Western sunrise.

CHAPTER X

BOOK COLLECTING

BY 1934 THE ROSENSTOCKS had outgrown their modest facility and obtained additional space in the adjoining building, which enabled them to double both the shelf area for books and the storage room. And, in 1936, the Rosenstock family expanded with the birth of their one and only child, Marilyn. Like the store, the apartment on Glenarm Street was no longer adequate, and shortly after the arrival of Marilyn they became involved in designing and building a new home in East Denver, one planned to accommodate Fred's extensive collections, and one in which he would live for at least another forty years.

It was also in 1934 that his "Western Americana" catalog was issued, although it was not confined entirely to Western items. L. J. Davidson, a professor at the University of Denver, wrote a brief introduction: ". . . Had there never existed the collector's passion, much of the source material for American History would have been permanently lost and many great libraries would lack their choicest possessions. The collector not only satisfies his own desire to possess rare and interesting works, he also builds up a legacy for those who, with increasing interest and in greater numbers, are turning to the study of our past as a means of enriching our present. This especially is true in regard to Western Americana; for, as has often been noted, the frontier has been the most American thing about America, and the story of the Indian adds a unique element to American history and literature."

In one sense, Fred was an innovator in his philosophy of collecting — or perhaps renegade would be a better word. The Anderson Galleries had been critical of his first offering for auction, complaining that he collected the extensive works of an author, contrary to the more accepted practice of collecting only one or two outstanding titles.

"Everybody," Fred pointed out, "was collecting the high spots of authors, so it was easier to collect those that weren't the high spots. But when you take an author like Longfellow, for instance, if you want to talk about the high spots only, all you would have would be perhaps *Evangeline* and maybe the *Courtship of Miles Standish,* and then you would have two books. I was interested in literature beyond the fact of just ordinary collecting. With my interest in Longfellow, if I would run into a first edition of one of his minor works (by comparison), and it was a good copy, I just couldn't walk away from it. If I could obtain it at a reasonable price, I'd feel compelled to buy it.

"And I felt that this business of limiting the collecting of any famous author or novelist or poet just from the standpoint of their high spots was not sound. I felt that an author ought to be represented by more than just one or two books. It might sometimes be the rarest book (and the most popular from the collector's point of view) but not necessarily the best book. So I refused to abide by the fact that the collecting of high spots was the thing to do."

Time has proven that, in terms of the thinking of today's literary scholars, Fred was right and the collectors of that day were wrong. Not only minor works but minor authors as well are sought after today.

To become a successful collector requires an extensive knowledge of the field, constant and comprehensive studying of catalogs and bibliographies; an extremely wide acquaintanceship among dealers and collectors; the nose of a thoroughbred well-trained to seek out the old and the rare; and a considerable amount of luck or, in the Rosenstock vernacular, "miracles."

His acquaintanceship with William C. Smith of Cincinnati led to the acquisition of some excellent items. Fred says, "I possibly bought the best things that Smith acquired outside of his Americana specialty (he had little interest in 'western' Americana). The only reason I did was because he took a liking to me." Proof of this warm relationship came not through the buying or selling of books, but under circumstances in which Fred needed financial help.

"I had sold the Bennett Book Studios in New York an almost complete set of the first editions of Herman Melville, including the first American edition of *Moby Dick,* a valuable book then and now. It turned out, four or five years later, that because of differences in binding this book I had supplied then came to be identified as a second issue. They weren't all bound up at once, and the theory was that this was probably a second binding.

"The customer who had bought the book from Bennett returned it, and Bennett made a claim on me. I really didn't feel I owed him anything, but my wife prevailed upon me. She said, 'Why have trouble with anybody? This man can talk about you and give you a black mark, or give people the impression that you aren't an honest dealer, and we don't want that.' This was during the depression, and I didn't have the money, but she insisted, 'Pay him and get him off your back.' The trouble was, I really didn't have any money at that particular time. All of a sudden I thought of Smith. He had been nice to me, and I didn't know who else to turn to. I wrote to Smith and explained the circumstances and, lo and behold, he sent me a check for $500 with a note, 'Pay me when you can.' I regard this today as one of the great favors that anyone ever did for me."

One facet of the art of book collecting is a natural talent for making friends among one's peers, a talent which Fred not only possessed but augmented by bestowing favors whenever possible. "About 1927, in Lowdermilk's in Washington," he recalls, "I bought a perfect, mint, pristine copy of the first issue of Walt Whitman's *Leaves of Grass.* It was one of my great finds in first editions — probably the finest copy in existence. It had all the points of the first edition — for example, the gold fillet lines on the covers. They didn't bind all of the edition at one time, and only the first bound had the gold fillet lines. Leaving out the gold fillet lines on the second binding made all the difference. Even though they were all printed at the same time, the second group to be bound became a second issue.

"I was excited about getting such an excessively rare first issue in such marvelous condition, and I would like to have kept it. But I sold it the next day to my great friend, the Whitman bibliographer and specialist in Whitman first editions, Alfred Goldsmith, who was also one of the outstanding dealers in New York. I could have sold it for more money elsewhere, but I felt this book should go to Alfred Goldsmith — and seeing the thrill he got at acquiring it was worth more than the price of the book."

Although the book collector must always be alert to opportunities, there is often the element of luck. Fred relates the experience of Frank Rosengren, his Chicago book-dealer friend. "He bought a collection of books, almost sight unseen, and felt it was mostly a bunch of junk, pamphlets, Congressional Record stuff, government reports. There was so much of it, and the few items he looked at were so unimpressive, that he packed it all up in cartons and stored them in his basement. He didn't look at the collection for five or six years.

"One weekend, for some reason I don't recall, he decided to go through the whole collection. What he found struck the attention of the whole bookloving and bookselling world, and it made all the papers, the news services. He had found, in that collection, a copy of the first edition of Poe's *Murders in the Rue Morgue,* bound up with about twenty completely insignificant items. At that time, as today, Poe is one of the most collected authors. And Poe volumes never lost value during the depression and he remains one of the most sought after as well as one of the most elusive authors. It was about 1935 when Rosengren found the volume — still the depression — and he sold it for $7,500 or $8,000. It was in good condition, but not an absolutely perfect copy. It was in some very small ways defective, like one corner of the title page missing."

For a collector, Fred's attitude toward first editions was a bit unusual. "As to first editions of Western Americana, those of us in the trade don't designate them by the term 'first edition.' We call them 'original editions.' Not only in the trade, but by most scholars and librarians they are referred to this way. Sometimes a reprint or a new edition is not merely a reprint; it may have new notes or other information. Often the original publication of a journal or diary was not edited at all and may have lots of errors in it, and later editions, perhaps the second, third, or even the tenth, have corrected such mistakes so that these later editions represent an important contribution. In fact, they might be better from the standpoint of conveying more accurate information.

"I take as much interest in a tenth edition, if it has the quality and contributes something to Americana, as in the first. There are libraries and individual collectors who feel that in buying the original edition of the book they have it like the author himself wanted it to be, perhaps that it represents more accurately his personal taste. Having the first edition, to some, it like the author himself was there in person, along with his book.

"I appreciate and understand that feeling, that desire for the original edition. Being historically minded, and with the respect that I have for the past and its true representation, I am thrilled with facets of a first edition. I handle it with reverence, and I do feel closer to the author, especially if I know he had something to do with the planning or design.

"When I examined that first edition of *Leaves of Grass,* which Walt Whitman actually helped to print, I had this feeling of intimacy that you don't get from a reprint, even though in some ways the reprint is the better book."

The successful collector and the rare book dealer must know far more than the fine points of a first edition; he must also accumulate a vast storehouse of information about the subject matter. With Fred Rosenstock, the subject ultimately was Western Americana. Perhaps one of the most important contacts and most influential guides in Fred's study of the West was Major Lester Gehman, who had one of the finest collections of Western Americana in the country by the time the first Rosenstock bookstore had opened. Gehman had been reading, studying, and collecting in that field since the early 1900s, and worked closely with Fred on his 1934 catalog. He knew, for example, the best account of the Lewis and Clark expeditions, about Rufus Sage's years in the Rocky Mountains, and the importance of Josiah Gregg's *Commerce of the Prairies*.

When it became apparent how valuable Major Gehman was to the Rosenstocks' acquisition, sales, and general education in the field of Western Americana, Fred eventually employed him. As questions arose, Gehman was available to respond to them, and Fred, always the student, absorbed and retained this fund of knowledge. As the 1930s wore on he came to feel quite at home with names of authors, titles of books, places and events in the West and felt prepared to venture out on his own in buying significant collections — always knowing that Major Gehman was only a phone call away.

In the late thirties, Fred and Nelson Goodman took frequent scouting trips by automobile into Texas and the midwest. Where one might find a collection was the unknown quantity, and Fred developed the talents of a news hawk, detective, and collector all rolled into one. "I went to a newspaper office in historic Vincennes, Indiana, owned by a Mrs. Emison. I told her I was a book seller looking for books on early American history and would like to contact families that might have books from several generations back. I asked her if she could give us the names of some of the descendants of pioneers who still lived in Vincennes, especially those who might have books.

"We did a bit of visiting, and she asked if I knew of any books on genealogy — particularly information on the Emison family, something she'd been looking for all her life. I made a note of it and when I returned to Denver started a search. It took me about two years to find such a book, but I finally did, bought it and sent it to her.

"She made us a list of eight families and put then in order of importance. We went to the first house and it was a bonanza. This family had books that must have belonged to their grandparents. The books were in the attic, hadn't been touched in years, many in shiny calf and other forms of leather binding, and just beautiful.

"There must have been between two and three hundred books in that attic, and they were nearly all on history. This would be called general Americana, the lives of revolutionary patriots, some Kentucky history, books relating to the Ohio River, and others on the Revolutionary War. Naturally, they were early history — from the middle 1700s up to 1820 or so. And all in good condition. The family was very receptive to the idea of selling these books, and were pleased with the four or five hundred dollars I gave them for a bunch of books that had just been gathering dust in their attic.

"Out of the eight names we only made three calls, and in every case we bought books. Mrs. Emison knew her people well, and everyone we talked to was receptive and wanted to sell. It was a good day, and both Nelson and I were pretty happy.

"The next day we arrived in Louisville, Kentucky, the only place where I had sent an ad ahead of time, so we went directly to the newspaper office — the *Louisville Courier Journal*. There was only one encouraging reply, from a Mrs. Zoeller, the widow of a prominent music dealer in Louisville. Her husband was interested in many facets of literature, and had a nice library of about fifteen hundred volumes. We didn't say in the ad that we were dealers — just cash buyers. In fact, she had written in response to the ad that she didn't want to sell to dealers. I talked to her on the phone and told her that I was a dealer, but also a *specialist* looking for certain books and suggested that if she would let me see what she had she might be surprised at what I would offer providing she had the books I was looking for.

"She explained to me later that she had had a bad experience with a dealer in Louisville and felt he had taken advantage of her. I reassured her that I had a good reputation and was a fair person. 'I'm not out to steal your books, only to buy them,' were the words I used. We went to her house and I began to point out what fine books she had, and she was impressed with my honesty. She fixed lunch for us and we spent almost the entire day there. The collection was miscellaneous, with books on oriental rugs, general Americana, music, good literature — probably one of the finest libraries in Louisville. I must have bought three to four hundred books from her and paid her about $1,500, a sizeable sum in the mid-thirties."

As the business grew, Fred did less and less scouting himself, but acquired the services of other book scouts or collector friends who would call to his attention private libraries and other hidden treasures. The depression years were a good time to acquire books, many people being forced to part with their personal collections to obtain cash. Fred did not pay commissions to his unofficial scouts but always made sure they were rewarded in some manner.

Two significant collections — the Pfeuffer library in New Braunfels, Texas, and a portion of the Dienst library in Temple, Texas — came to Fred's attention in 1938. Frank Caldwell, a collector from Austin, had advised Fred that the Pfeuffer family would be interested in discussing the sale of the library, and Fred began negotiations. In December, with Nelson Goodman on vacation from medical school, it was decided that they would drive to Texas and examine the collections.

The Pfeuffer family had originally come to Texas from Germany in the 1840s and had been acquiring books, not only in the English language, but also in German, French, and Spanish, for three generations. Fortunately, from Fred's point of view, the fourth generation was not interested in adding to or even retaining the collection.

Fred examined the collection in a warehouse where it had remained for years gathering dust. The library consisted of about three thousand books, pamphlets, and early imprints related to Texas. After Fred had purchased the library, he offered Caldwell the opportunity to select fifty or sixty books gratis, and gave him first purchase rights, at bargain prices, on forty additional items. In total, for his efforts in calling this collection to Fred Rosenstock's attention, Caldwell obtained about a hundred of the best books. But it was such a rich treasure that it could withstand such a raid without being seriously crippled.

Once the Pfeuffer transaction had been consummated, Fred and Nelson drove to Temple and very quickly made arrangements to buy the remaining portion of the Dienst library. Earl Vandale, the noted Texas collector, had acquired some of the manuscript material in this collection a short time earlier. "It's the kind of business," Fred stresses, "where you have to take advantage of opportunities. If you decide to wait until times are better, or until you're in a better cash position, most of the time you lose the real treasures — those that separate you from the less successful dealers."

Even before Fred had opened the boxes that came from Texas, Earl Vandale had arrived on the scene. Fred had spent an evening with him on his recent buying trip, and Vandale was anxious to see Fred's purchases and wanted the first chance to select from the Pfeuffer collection.

There were approximately seventy-five cartons of books on Texas and the Southwest, and Fred had hoped to go through the shipment, select the more significant items and put a price on them. But Earl Vandale was in the store and impetuously began to open the boxes himself and make selections on the spot. Fred explained that he didn't know what prices to put on the books. Vandale responded that *he* knew the books so Fred shouldn't be concerned.

"It was a grueling experience," Fred recalls, "not having any knowledge of the important Texas items at the time. I was completely in Vandale's hands." He selected about two hundred books and offered $3,500 for them. Fred was certain they were worth considerably more, but agreed, partly because of his admiration for Vandale's perseverance as a collector.

Like Vandale, Fred was endowed with the qualities of tenacity and persistence. Early in the thirties Fred became acquainted with three executives of the Denver and Rio Grande Railroad — R. F. Weitbrec, Frank Wadleigh, and George Beam — all Denver residents and all with fine libraries, particularly rich in early Colorado imprints. Eventually he acquired all three libraries, although twenty years passed before he finally obtained the Beam collection.

While the acquisition of collections was perhaps the most important way to strengthen his holdings, Fred also sought out individual items or the complete papers and journals of a single individual who may have been significant in the annals of Western history.

Kit Carson, trapper, guide, soldier of the West, played a vital role in the early development of America, particularly in northern New Mexico and southern Colorado. There have been several Carson biographies, but, Fred notes, "the one 'Life' that is still generally regarded as the most comprehensive and basic, and from which all succeeding biographies have necessarily copied, is the famous work, *Kit Carson Days,* published originally in 1914."

Edwin L. Sabin, the Colorado author, began his study for the definitive life of Carson about 1894. "At that time," Fred points out, "there were yet many men and women alive who knew Carson; particularly some who served with him during the Civil War and in the Navajo campaigns in the Southwest. Sabin did a stupendous job of research on Carson. Talk about present-day biographers and historians who turn them out fast! Sabin labored twenty years on the project and in that time was able to gather nearly every scrap of information on Carson from first-hand 'reporters' who knew him from every angle."

In the mid-1930s, Sabin wrote Fred from California to ask if he would be interested in buying the many letters and other bits of information that had represented the "working materials" for the Carson study. "Would I! Of course I replied in the affirmative and with enthusiasm. But we were in the heart of a depression and I said, frankly, that I did not believe I could afford such a choice morsel. Sabin said, 'Don't worry, you'll be able to afford it,' and he set the price — one that I could afford. By today's standards I shudder to think what I might be asked to pay for such a collection.

"I've been on the prowl for Carson material ever since, and I have found some wonderful things. For instance, I acquired an original daguerreotype of Carson taken in his better years, when he was healthy and plump; not emaciated as he was in his last days, after being beseiged by illness." In the picture Carson had the young son of Tom Boggs, his close friend and patron, on his knee. Fred acquired it as part of the Beam collection.

It is surprising how many people discard old, rare, and often valuable books. During the early years of the Bargain Book Store, Fred contacted such organizations as the Salvation Army, the Veterans' Salvage House and St. Vincent de Paul. The Goodwill Industries, in the thirties, had an arrangement with another book dealer, Meyer Kramer, a good friend of the Rosenstocks. The Kramers and Rosenstocks frequently went out together and played bridge together. Fred and Frances accompanied Meyer and his wife on fishing trips, although Fred never fished, content to be an interested observer. In 1939, Stasia Kramer became ill and at her doctor's suggestion they moved to California. Fred agreed to purchase the Kramers' bookstore with the understanding that should they return to Denver he would sell it back to them at the same price Fred paid for it.

"About a year later they came back and I returned the store to Kramer. But by the end of 1940 his wife's condition worsened and they left again. I bought out his stock, but not the store, and took over his arrangement with Goodwill." Every week Fred and his assistant would go to the Goodwill warehouse and examine all the books which had come in, classifying them into different types, setting aside those of particular interest.

It was a mutual aid society, with Fred advising them as to which books were of no value, which were mediocre, and which were significant collectors' items. The books of no particular significance were sold by Goodwill for twenty-five cents each, but the better books Fred would price for them on an individual basis.

Titles relating to Americana would be sold to the Bargain Book Store, usually for thirty or forty dollars for the lot, although on one visit he found a copy of Mathews's *Pencil Sketches of Colorado,* in rather poor condition, and he paid Goodwill $75.00 for the volume. He continued his arrangement with Goodwill for about ten years, giving it up after a new director took over the organization. About the same time, with the pressures at the bookstore increasing and more opportunities coming his way, he discontinued all of his contacts with the salvage houses. "It would never make a dealer rich," Fred emphasized, "but it was a challenge and a thrill to discover even one good book."

Perhaps it was this intangible excitement — the lust of the hunt — that provided that extra ingredient separating the great from the near-great in the book collectors' arena. These were not merely books to Fred Rosenstock; they were alive, and to collect these treasures was an experience. In his 1934 catalog, he writes: "Many of these rarities represent thrilling adventure in their acquisition; and the process of packing off some pamphlet to a person in Rhode Island will at once bring the thought, 'I'd like to tell him how many times my heart was in my mouth coming down that slippery, wet, narrow mountain road that night, with the brakes "on the blink," to Breckenridge and back; all for that pamphlet.' In the spare West, where old families are few and distances far between, the hunt for rare books is more exciting even if more laborious."

CHAPTER XI

FORTUNE HUNTING

EXCEPT FOR OCCASIONAL, isolated intervals — his early romance with Jeannette Stadler, his confinement at the Oakes Rest Home, his courtship of Frances — Fred Rosenstock devoted virtually all of his time and energy to his business ventures, whether it was selling billboards, peddling real estate or insurance programs, or dealing in books, and later, investing in Western art.

During 1935–36, when Frances was pregnant, it became necessary to plan and build a new home. But Fred's participation was minimal. It was his brother-in-law, Nelson Goodman, who did most of the shopping for the new furniture as the moving day approached. "I'd have to say," his daughter Marilyn reflects, "that they were sort of weekend parents." From her earliest recollection until she was able to take care of herself, both her father and mother worked long hours at the bookstore and hired a housekeeper to handle the domestic chores and look after Marilyn.

She cherished those rare occasions spent with her father. "He would take me to Mammoth Gardens to watch the boxing matches and lady wrestlers. And he always loved baseball, and the two of us sometimes went to see the Denver Bears. In fact, we went often enough that I learned the names of the players."

Family vacations were likewise infrequent. Frances enjoyed the hot mineral water at Eldorado Springs and Glenwood Springs, both resorts located in the mountains about a hundred miles from Denver, and mother and daughter would occasionally spend a week or two swimming and hiking, but Fred never was with them for more than a weekend.

While interested in spectator sports, Fred avoided most outdoor activities, preferring a poker game now and then with his book dealer companions. The Rosenstocks and the Kramers were close friends, and Meyer Kramer made several attempts to introduce Fred to the joys of the outdoors. "We used to go on fishing trips with the Kramers," Marilyn recalls, "and they tried to get my father to fish. He'd trudge along beside Mr. Kramer, and sit on the bank of the stream and talk — but he never fished.

"My uncle, Nelson Goodman, liked to go rabbit hunting and once in a while would get my father to go along. They'd speed through the fields, Nelson driving, with my father outside on the running board looking for the rabbits. I'm sure he never shot one. He never killed anything in his life."

One of the high points in Marilyn's adolescence — and a significant event in Fred's career as well — was a trip to California in 1951, when Marilyn was fifteen. "It was one of the few times that we were together on a vacation — even though it was a business-vacation for my father, as were all the vacations he took. We flew to Albuquerque — it was my Dad's first flight — and met Frank Waters and had a long visit with him. The next day Homer Britzman, a friend of my father's who lived in Los Angeles, arrived to drive us to California. He had a brand new Packard and was a very fast driver and a heavy drinker. Every time we'd stop for gas Mr. Britzman would have another drink. While they were driving my father would argue with him about prices for paintings and other things. Just to irritate him. Later he told me he did it on purpose just to keep Mr. Britzman awake. But he gave us the grand tour — the Painted Desert, Petrified Forest, the rim of the Grand Canyon, Meteor Crater. It really was an exciting journey."

Britzman owned "Trails End," the house that Charles Russell had built in Pasadena, which was completed the year he died. Russell's widow lived there until her death in 1939, when Britzman purchased it.

The Rosenstocks were his houseguests, and Marilyn was tremendously impressed. "It was filled with Russell paintings. There were all kinds of little alcoves and special lighting — designed to show off his work. My father had been collecting Russells off and on for years, but I think this was the real beginning of his Russell collection. He bought a lot of paintings while we were at Britzman's house.

"Britzman was very jealous of my father's time and felt that since he had driven us to California and we were staying at his house that we shouldn't go anywhere without him. My father couldn't resist bookstores, and he took off one day for Los Angeles and didn't get back to the house until very late. Homer Britzman had locked him out of the house. Somehow my father managed to get in, but all of the light switches were behind paintings and there was much stumbling and fumbling in the dark before he finally got to his bedroom."

Eventually everybody considered it as a joke, and Fred and Marilyn spent another enjoyable two or three days at Britzman's home before taking a bus to San Francisco to visit relatives and friends.

"But then we had our first real vacation. Some friends took us to Yosemite — my father and me. We were late starting, and it was one o'clock in the morning when we arrived at the park. The Smiths — our friends — had brought a tent and we tried to put it up in the dark, and it was finally erected enough for us to sleep in. The next morning we looked out and saw that we were practically on the front steps of National Park Headquarters. We stayed at Yosemite for four or five days, doing all the tourist things — riding bicycles, seeing the sights. Even then, my father would manage to find a phone and call the store every day to see what was happening."

In 1956 his daughter, then a student at the University of Colorado in Boulder, wrote an essay for a creative writing course in which she related some of the incidents in her father's life. "In 1938 he had been corresponding with Dr. Francis W. Cragin, a retired history professor living in Colorado Springs, having learned from a book dealer in Kansas City that Dr. Cragin had an extensive library." An appointment was finally set up for ten o'clock on a Sunday morning, and Fred went to the Springs, arriving — as was his habit — right on time, only to see the old professor leaving his house.

"I thought we had an appointment at ten o'clock," Fred said.

"Just wait awhile, young fellow," the professor replied, continuing on his way. "I'll talk to you when I get back from church."

Fred was understandably upset and was about to let his pride get the best of him when he noticed a rather valuable book — a copy of *Uncle Dick Wootton* — being used as a doorstop for the front door. Fred reconsidered, thinking that if the professor used such a rare book for a doorstop what might he have inside the house?

They agreed to meet two hours later outside the church. Again Fred's patience was tested, as the eccentric gentleman insisted that they have lunch at a particular restaurant. Fred agreed, his irritation surpassed only by his curiosity. Marilyn writes: "Finally my father was allowed to see the books. The collection was much better than even his greatest expectations. His desire to buy the books was so intense that the offer he made on the collection was higher than it should have been. Therefore he was absolutely astounded when the old man said, 'I've decided not to sell you the books.'

"This was altogether unexpected, and my father's only reply was, 'Why in the devil did you ask me to come here in the first place?'

"What my father didn't know was that the old man had been writing a history of the West. . . . He had been gathering his material for a long time without collecting any money for his efforts. His debts now amounted to several thousand dollars, including a past due mortgage payment on his house. He had considered selling his books so that he could pay his bills. Actually he still planned to finish his history and didn't want to part with the material he needed for his research.

"After much haggling, my father finally consented to a deal which no businessman in his right mind should accept. He agreed to pay the old man $3,500 for the collection immediately, but would not receive the major items in the collection for one year, which Dr. Cragin thought

Fred and Marilyn, age three, on a mountain vacation

would be sufficient time to complete his research and finish writing his history."

The professor was past eighty, visibly in fragile health, and "during the following year my father made monthly visits to Colorado Springs to make sure that the old man was still alive. . . . These visits were rather strange. My father would take him to lunch and then they would listen to baseball games on the radio. There was never any conversation between them except for a few comments about the ball game.

"At last the year ended, and my father received the books as he had been promised, without the slightest protest on the part of the professor. As for Dr. Cragin, he died a few months later without completing his history of the West. The notes and material he collected, however, thanks to my father, are still being used by historians today and are housed in the Colorado Springs Pioneer Museum."

Another incident in the life of this book-collecting fortune hunter involved a mountain man, Philander Simmons. In Marilyn's words, "Simmons traveled with the famous trapper and mountain man, Old Bill Williams, and his diary contained firsthand accounts of early days in the West. My father had acquired Philander Simmons' original diary and was interested in publishing a book about the man.

"A friend of my father's, Frederic Voelker, who lived in St. Louis, was an authority on Bill Williams and agreed to write the book. Philander Simmons' diary was to be the basis for the book, but many parts of it did not seem to agree with known historical facts. . . . My father and Mr. Voelker concluded that the last part of the diary must have been written when Simmons was a very old man and his memory had conceivably dimmed. This meant further research was required to fill in the blanks and correct the inconsistencies. Consequently my father was eager to learn of anyone who might have known Simmons or who might have access to any old photographs or letters concerning him.

"Possible information about Simmons came from a rather unexpected source. My uncle, Dr. Harry Goodman, then a dentist in Pueblo, Colorado, happened to be visiting us one weekend. When my father mentioned the Philander Simmons' affair, my uncle suddenly expressed interest. 'I think I know someone who might have been acquainted with the old boy,' my uncle said. 'There's an old hermit who comes to my office every once in a while. He lives up in the mountains with only his horse to keep him company. He's a trapper — that's how he gets enough money to live.'

"My uncle managed to get directions to the old man's shack, located in the foothills near Rye, Colorado, and a date was set for an attempt to find and meet him. Fred Voelker had come to town, also eager to see the hermit. So one morning in October my father, my uncle and his son, and Mr. Voelker started out to find the fur trapper. The directions were imprecise, and the dirt road which supposedly was in the vicinity of his cabin eventually became impassable for a car. So they started to walk. It had been snowing and the ground was slick, the terrain rugged and abounding with deep gullies. My father was more of a city man than an outdoorsman and found the long hike difficult and exasperating. But, with the promise of treasure ahead, he hopped across the gullies without a word of complaint."

About the time they were discussing giving up the search, a horse appeared out of one of the gullies and started trotting toward a nearby hill. The group spied a lean-to protecting the entrance to a dilapidated shack built in a cave-like opening in the base of the hillside.

"The hermit greeted the intruders with suspicion, but became more friendly when he saw the man who had relieved him of several miserable toothaches." After a few minutes of small talk he led Fred and his friends to an outbuilding, inside of which were hanging an assortment of skins and furs of animals.

"In a moment of questionable good humor (precarious, my father thought), my uncle pointed to Fred Voelker and said, 'This is a fur trader from St. Louis.' Actually, Mr. Voelker knew nothing about furs.

" 'Well,' said the hermit, 'if you're really a fur expert, what kind of fur is this?' He pointed to a nondescript grayish-brown pelt.

"Fred Voelker, innocently put on the spot, stared at the fur and then at my uncle, concerned that the hermit might not be too happy over being deceived. Finally, with some trepidation but with a show of bravado, he exclaimed, 'It's cat.'

"After a momentary pause the hermit smiled and said, 'You're right. You certainly know your furs.' The two of them shook hands, and the crisis was over.

"But my Dad wanted to talk business and asked the trapper, 'Did you ever know Philander Simmons, or did you ever hear of Bill Williams?'

" 'Well,' began the hermit, 'I've known so many mountain men in my time — and it was so long ago — no, can't say as I remember either of them. But then again, I *might* have known Simmons.'

"My father was irritated and disappointed, thanked the hermit for his hospitality and promised to send him a copy of the book on Philander Simmons when it was published. But it was a promise my father never fulfilled, because the book was never published."

Marilyn relates another incident that occurred in 1955, and was the one and only time that she thought her father had made a mistake in the book collecting business. En route to California by train, she and her father stopped for a day in Provo, Utah, while Fred visited with a close friend and professor of history at Brigham Young University. "The professor," Marilyn writes, "suggested that my father talk to a man, also a BYU professor, who had a fine collection of rare Mormon items. After spending most of the day looking at this library, my father returned empty-handed. 'There was only one item I wanted,' he told me, 'but the man wanted too much money for it.'

"We were ready to board the train for California — in fact my father had one hand on the handrail — when we saw a man running full speed toward us. It was the professor who owned the rare book my father had wanted. He slipped a small volume into my father's pocket. 'Take it,' he said, 'we'll argue about the price later.'

"As the train raced toward Salt Lake City, my father thumbed through the book. Suddenly I noticed that he was frowning. 'What's wrong?' I asked. 'How can such a little book disturb you so much?'

"He proceeded to tell me about the book. 'This rare Mormon item is the *Book of Commandments* and was published in 1833 in "Zion," which was actually Independence, Missouri. This particular copy belonged to, and had the bookplates of David Whitmer, who was one of the witnesses to Joseph Smith's original finding of the golden plates — on which the Mormon religion is largely based.'

"My father observed that each of the verses in the book ended with the word 'Amen.' The last verse of the book, however, did not end with 'Amen.' In fact, the book had no ending. 'This is a defective copy,' my father concluded. When we arrived in Salt Lake, he tried to call the person who had sold him the book to tell him that he would not buy a defective volume. But he was unable to reach him, and we continued on to San Francisco.

"Some friends were waiting for us, but my father had only one thing on his mind. 'Please take me to Howell's [bookstore]. I want to check the bibliographical record of a certain item.' Unfortunately it was very late in the day and Howell's had just closed. But he was back on the hunt first thing in the morning, and he finally found the data he needed on the *Book of Commandments*. When he walked out of the bookstore there was a broad grin on his face.

" 'I wasn't deceived after all,' he said. 'The book was published incomplete. It seems that while the book was being printed, an anti-Mormon mob attacked the printing office, and the machinery as well as most of the copies of the book were destroyed. What few survived were issued incomplete — in exactly the state they happened to be at that moment.' "

The one aspect of the book business that Fred enjoyed more than any other was the search for and discovery of a rare volume or a significant collection or private library that had been overlooked. One such collection, that conceivably might have been lost to the historic and literary world, was the private library of Jefferson Davis, the president of the Confederacy.

Some of Davis's descendants moved to Colorado Springs after the

Civil War, bringing with them the extensive assemblage of books he had gathered, as well as various letters and some original music manuscripts composed by Davis's wife Varina.

"It was obviously a great find, and I purchased the collection from the great-grandchildren who were still living in Colorado Springs. Then I worked hard for about ten years to supplement the original acquisition, adding at least a hundred more items during that time.

"When I felt I had gone as far as I could in my effort to restore the Davis Library, I could have approached some well-funded university or the Library of Congress and probably made a handsome profit. But I chose to do the historically and sentimentally correct thing and offered it to the State of Mississippi practically at my cost. But Mississippi is not a wealthy state, and Governor Coleman himself called to tell me that before they could purchase it the legislature would have to vote the funds. He asked if I'd be willing to wait until the lawmakers convened. I waited — but they turned down the proposition. So he asked if I could wait another year, convinced that he could get the appropriation at the next session. Maybe it wasn't good business practice, but I agreed to go along for another year. They finally appropriated the funds and the Davis Library is now where it belongs, at the Memorial Building in Jackson, Mississippi, along with other Jefferson Davis mementos."

Placed near the entrance to the collection is this inscription on parchment: "The books in the library of the Confederate President and his family. The depth of his intelligence and the breadth of interests are reflected in the wide range of subjects here. Books of biography and history, next to the Bible and Book of Common Prayer, were his favorites. Sir Walter Scott, Lord Byron, and other romantics, share shelf space with science, natural history, music, philosophy, and religion.

"The decoration of the room is not an attempt at beauty, or grace, but is based on photographs and sketches of the Davis study as it was, cluttered with the books of a talented and cultural family, and with the souvenirs of a significant American career."

A mere handful of people who read that parchment and admire the

Davis collection are aware that had it not been for a Fred Rosenstock this important remnant of the American heritage might have been forever lost.

Usually, as in the case of the discovery of the Jefferson Davis library, the excitement results from the significance of the collection. But there have been times in Fred's life when the circumstances of the search were more important than the treasure he uncovered.

In 1969 a young man walked into the Rosenstock bookstore with a copy of Mathews's *Pencil Sketches of Colorado* under his arm. He had been offered a few hundred dollars for it by a dealer in Colorado Springs. "It wasn't a real good copy," Fred notes, "and would probably bring about $2,000." Fred offered him $1,200 and the young man was very pleased. It was then that the real story was revealed, a remarkable chain of events that started in 1922 when Fred was struggling to survive at the Denver Book Shop.

Robert S. Ellison, who eventually became the president of the Midwest Refining Company, had accumulated one of the finest private libraries in the West and was one of Fred's earliest customers. He was an astute buyer, and the young bookman at that time was outmatched. "I remember selling him a copy of *Banditti of the Plains,* probably one of the rarest books I had, for five dollars. It's now worth $500."

Ellison and Fred became good friends, and he was a frequent visitor at the Bargain Book Store after his retirement from the oil business. He moved to Colorado Springs and purchased the rambling Bell Mansion — one of the more lavish historic homes in the Colorado Springs–Manitou area. Fred was an occasional visitor at the mansion, located on spacious grounds so close to the mountains that deer often wandered into the yard from their high retreats.

In 1947, a week or so after Ellison's last visit to the Rosenstock store, he was stricken ill and died quite suddenly. In the ambulance on the way to the hospital, Ellison talked to his wife Vida about the disposition of his library, which had not been mentioned in his will, and asked that it be donated to his alma mater, the University of Indiana.

With Fred's knowledge and reputation, as well as his long association with Ellison, it was logical that the administrators of the estate requested Fred to appraise the library. Accompanied by Major Gehman, Fred spent a week at the Ellison home, not only evaluating the books for tax purposes, but assisting Vida in determining which volumes should be sent to Indiana and which she might retain. She wanted to keep the Colorado, Wyoming, Custer, and Northwest materials, and Fred separated these and arranged them for her. Even though the major part of the collection went to the University, the original library was so extensive that Mrs. Ellison still retained a substantial bibliotheca.

Vida Ellison died in 1967, willing the library to her sister who lived in a small mountain town, Florissant, some twenty miles west of Colorado Springs. "The mansion was sold and the books were crated and sent to Florissant," Fred relates. "Then, months later I heard that the sister died, but there was no phone and I hadn't given it any more thought until this young man, Mr. Fallis, came into the store.

"After I had purchased the Mathews book, he revealed that his parents, neighbors of Vida Ellison's sister, had taken care of her during her last years and illness, and that they had been willed the Ellison books; also that they now wished to sell them. I arranged to go to Florissant the following Sunday, and for the next eight weeks I was there — every Sunday, the only day I could get away — to go over the collection. The books were stored in long, wooden boxes, coffin-like, in a barn several hundred feet from the house. It was winter, there was no heat, and the light was bad. I went through every item and made an individual bid on each book." The Fallises sold him the entire collection, including many books that Fred had once sold Robert Ellison some thirty or forty years earlier.

Having one of the most complete libraries on Western Americana that could ever be found in a bookstore, Fred eventually became known, not only to collectors, but to the Western writer as well. The list of authors who have wandered among shelves is endless: Irving Stone, Frank Dobie, David Lavender, James Michener, Frank Waters.

J. Frank Dobie, while not a collector in the technical sense, put together, says J. E. Reynolds, a noted bookseller, "with loving care the greatest collection of books on the range livestock industry ever assembled by a private individual in this country." Dobie bought books from the Rosenstocks for many years, usually writing a letter and attaching a list of the titles he was looking for.

In 1952 Fred arranged a lecture tour for Dobie that included the University of Colorado, the University of Denver, Colorado State University and Colorado State College at Greeley. "About five hundred people attended his talk at the University of Denver," Fred recalls, "and his subject was on the psychology of Western animals — mostly the coyote. The lecture lasted one hour, but he was so fascinating it could have gone on all night. The audience was mesmerized. I remember that he had a big pocket watch, like the railroad men used to use, and he would pull that out and look at it from time to time. He stopped on the dot of one hour and no amount of applause could make him go on."

After Dobie returned to Texas he wrote an article for the *San Antonio Light,* in which he referred to Fred Rosenstock's Bargain Book Store: "It is crammed with old books, some very rare. . . . A person can learn an enormous amount by looking through books that he does not actually read. I incline to judge the civilization of a city by its bookstores — or by their absence. A genuine bookstore is far more than a house of merchandise. As an asset of civilization, it is in the same category as public libraries."

About 1954 Irving Stone started to write *Men to Match My Mountains,* a classic history of the opening of the West between 1840–1900, with particular emphasis on the role of mining in the development of this frontier. Stone knew the history of California, and had no problem with obtaining Nevada material, but his knowledge of Colorado mining was slim. Someone suggested he contact Fred Rosenstock, and he came to Denver and started prowling around the Bargain Book Store. He started picking books off the shelf — perhaps twenty or thirty. He wanted to buy some of them, but not all. Those with limited material of interest he wanted to borrow. Fred told him to take whatever he needed and return them when he was finished — at no charge.

Not long after that episode, Fred and Marilyn flew to California and Irving Stone met them at the airport and took them to his home in Beverly Hills. His wife was away, but Stone donned an apron and cooked breakfast for the two of them. The noted author talked of books with Fred, but with even more enthusiasm showed him his extensive collection of pre-Columbian art.

Fred's association with New Mexico's Frank Waters goes back many years, and he agrees with the authorities and scholars that Waters is one of America's most brilliant writers on Western subjects, particularly Indians and the Southwest. Fred attended a meeting of the Arizona Historical Society in Tucson shortly before Waters's *Book of the Hopi* was released, and Frank Waters was the main speaker. As Fred looked at this tall, gaunt figure with his lean, weathered face, sunken cheeks, and penetrating eyes that almost sparkled when he talked, the bookman was suddenly struck with Waters's resemblance to Lincoln. After the meeting, while talking about the wonderful world of books, Fred mentioned this, and Frank admitted that others had commented on the similarity. "Of course, Frank didn't have Lincoln's beard," Fred noted. Waters has a large following, many visitors who feel, when meeting him, that they should bow as before a shrine. "I get a lot of people in the store from all over the country who tell me, 'Frank Waters says if anyone has this book, you'll have it.'"

David Lavender, a superb craftsman in the field of writing Western history, recalls that "it was late in the 1940s that I first started dropping into the old Bargain Book Store to buy books when I could afford them (when I couldn't Fred would generally knock down the price to the point where there was almost no profit left for himself) and just to talk about Western Americana in general. . . . What I have is an impression of a volatile, excitable, enthusiastic, generous man to whom conversation about the things he loved was the savor of life — a rare and wonderful soul."

CHAPTER XII

PUBLISHING THE WEST

———— ∞∞∞∞∞ ————

BY THE SUMMER OF 1940 when Hitler was snuffing out the lights of freedom in France and a number of shortsighted Americans were expounding the policy of isolation across the land, Fred A. Rosenstock was forty-five years old and had been in the book business off and on for fifteen years. During that period he had not only accumulated a significant collection of books relating to the West, but also a substantial number of unpublished items, such as journals, diaries, miscellaneous papers and documents, and some art.

From time to time, as he read and studied the diaries and other accounts written in the sometimes undecipherable scrawl of an early pioneer, he recognized that some of this material was not only interesting, but filled significant gaps in the history of the West. "Why," he wondered, "should this material be confined to the collector or the occasional researcher, when it could be published and become an important part of our heritage?" In the beginning, the idea of publishing books himself was a somewhat nebulous, passing thought.

But that was before his Number One Miracle — as Fred prefers to call it — that started when he was reading some rare copies of the *Western Literary Messenger* (which he had obtained as part of the Sabin Collection on Kit Carson) and noted a reference to a Warren Ferris. "Ferris," Fred related in a talk to the Denver Posse of the Westerners in 1965, "was a young man of an impetuous nature, living in Buffalo, New York, in the 1820s. After an insignificant family argument he wandered westward and after a time found himself in the frontier town of St.

[141]

Louis in 1829, jobless and dejected. Luckily, he learned the American Fur Company was preparing a fur trapping expedition to the Rocky Mountains. Ferris's knowledge and general intelligence won him a place on the expedition — as clerk."

He recorded his experiences that extended over four years in a diary, "a veritable saga of the mountain men, embodying hair-raising adventure, Indian fighting, life-and-death competition with other fur trading parties. Ferris's narrative, among many remarkable episodes, records a glowing account — one of the very first — of the wonders of the Yellowstone." Ferris attempted to have his account published by one of the leading publishers, without success. Finally a younger brother arranged for it to be published serially in an obscure Buffalo weekly paper, *The Western Literary Messenger,* during 1842–43. Fred had obtained only a few odd issues, some of which had installments of the Ferris diary. "My interest aroused, I began a systematic survey, writing to libraries and archives all over the country in an effort to gather a complete set of the pertinent issues of the *Western Literary Messenger.*" Fred had decided that, if he could put the entire narrative together, he would publish it. "Since I had done so much to bring all of the pieces together, I wanted to have the joy of putting it out for the first time in published form."

After a search that lasted many months, he had located all but sixteen issues. "I had arranged with a very knowledgeable and capable editor, Dr. Paul Phillips, historian of the University of Montana at Missoula, to edit a published book of the Ferris story. Dr. Phillips felt he could at least partially fill the gaps, or missing portions, by means of well-considered presuppositions and documented notes.

"Dr. Phillips began to work on Ferris, under this plan. I undertook to trace down Ferris's later career, in Texas, where he spent the balance of his life until his death in 1873. . . . Having fathered twelve children, there were scads of Ferrises all over Texas, and two daughters were still alive, in their late eighties. Strangely, however, even though Ferris was a professional photographer himself in his later years, no likeness of him was ever found."

The miracle continues with the appearance of a young man by the name of Schwab at the Bargain Book Store, "searching for runs of serials — in other words, magazines in sequence. . . ." Fred had a long run of the *Southwest Historical Quarterly* along with others that the customer purchased. "When we concluded our business, I asked him to lunch . . . and while eating our sandwiches young Mr. Schwab tells me he is from Boston, does not have a bookstore, only a warehouse where he keeps his stock of old magazines, and that his business is done entirely by catalog.

" 'Do you want to see what my catalog looks like?' asks Schwab, as he pulls out a rather unimposing mimeographed list of about a dozen pages. 'This list doesn't go to booksellers at all,' he says. 'It is sent only to libraries which are my principal customers.'

"Mainly out of courtesy, I aimlessly turn the pages of Schwab's catalog when, lo and behold (I could have missed this easily, under the circumstances) I see the words, *Western Literary Messenger!* With a quickened heartbeat I exclaim, 'What's this?'

" 'Oh,' he answers, 'just a big bound volume of an old newspaper. Nothing special about it.'

"With great trepidation I ask, 'Do you still have this?' "

Schwab assured the excited book dealer that he did, but also advised him that he was on his honeymoon and wouldn't be returning to Boston for some time. Over the young man's protest, Fred insisted on paying for the volume at once and then explained the reason for his eagerness.

"Nearly three months later a big package came. Would it hold the answer to our prayer . . . ? Feverishly I rip the outside wrapper and a large bound volume of *Western Literary Messenger* comes into view. I begin to turn the pages with caution; then faster. . . . Joy and excitement sweep over me. 'Eureka! Look here, everybody!' I cry. 'We have Ferris complete!' Every single chapter was there. It flashed through my mind that Edward Eberstadt, the renowned New York dealer in Americana, had once told me if the complete Ferris journal was ever found, he would be the one to locate it."

But that was not the end of the Ferris miracle. Some weeks later

Fred was casually looking at a publication called "Want List," in which booksellers and libraries listed specific wants, when he noticed an advertisement by a New York book-search service for issues of the *Western Literary Messenger* and several other related ephemeral items, "the combination of which, to me, meant only one thing: they are looking for material on Ferris!"

Fred's reaction was immediate. "I must head them off," knowing what a fiasco it could be if someone else was planning a book on Ferris. He wrote to the advertiser, the American Library Service, advising them that he was preparing to publish a book on Ferris which would be out "in a matter of weeks." He heard nothing from American Library Service. "About a month later, Dr. Phillips, in Missoula, receives a letter from a Walter McCausland, the 'client' himself, in whose behalf the ad was placed. McCausland turns out to be an engineer in Buffalo — Ferris's home town — a stamp collector who, in his rambles and his hobby-hunting for old stamps and covers, had the extreme good fortune to run into an immense batch of old letters of the Ferris family — these letters being one hundred years old at the time. McCausland further relates to Phillips, 'I have several letters written by Warren Ferris from the far West to his family in Buffalo,' and (wonder of wonders) 'I also have a map, drawn by Ferris, which is titled, *Map of the Fur Country.*' This was the bombshell! To my knowledge none of the old mountain men or fur traders had ever drawn such a map of this vast, scantily explored region, with the possible exception of the so-called *Colter Map,* and that wasn't really drawn by Colter. . . ."

Both Fred and Dr. Phillips agreed that the Ferris volume had to include that map, though it would mean delaying the publication. However, McCausland was reluctant to part with the map, since he planned to use it in a genealogical work on the Ferris family as a contribution to early Buffalo history. "I wrote, wired, cajoled, shed tears — and finally I succeeded in convincing McCausland that the Ferris map belonged with the Ferris narrative. Not only did he consent to my reproducing this unusual map in our book, but he became a most enthusiastic collaborator, permitting us to include some of Ferris's original letters with our book.

"... When the book finally came out, in 1940, it was heralded by historians everywhere. Something of the 'story within the story' — the evolution of unusual incidents that happened along the way — hit the newspapers, with the result that all the national news services of the time . . . ran special features on the subject, and altogether . . . about eight hundred newspapers over the country used the story."

With the Old West Publishing Company off to such an auspicious beginning, there was little doubt that Fred Rosenstock would continue his publishing operations. He had a wealth of material, although — as in the case of the Ferris narrative — gaps, inconsistencies or lack of complete identification frequently required extensive research before Fred felt the project was ready for publication. But the primary difficulty, in his words, "was that I had never found the right person to fill the role of editor. I have things today I probably will never publish for that reason. Every time I want to do a book, I match up this person (the editor) with the nature of the manuscript."

Fred's method of operating a publishing business was hardly conventional. The author (editor)-publisher relationship was based on faith, mutual confidence, and a close, personal rapport once a project was under way. "I never signed a contract," Fred says. "Our agreements, as author and publisher, were always verbal. Dale Morgan reminded me of this once, reflecting on our relationship and complimenting the pair of us for having had such a long relationship without a written agreement."

While it is not possible to generalize concerning his operation, since each book had its unique qualities not only in contrast and format, but in the circumstances surrounding its origin and development. S. Lyman Tyler, close personal friend of Fred's and for many years director of the Brigham Young University Library, describes the conception of a new book: "Once I was with Fred in the old Bargain Book Store during the small hours after midnight selecting books for the Brigham Young University Library. Fred was anticipating the arrival of Kenneth Sender, a book scout and dealer who concentrated considerable effort in the mid-west region, and frequently brought in unusual and valuable material. He arrived about two or three A.M., which was customary, for he knew Fred would normally be there at that time, and that then they would not be disturbed by the telephone or questions from customers.

"On this occasion, along with considerable additional material, he brought a diary written by a woman traveling with her new husband and others from Keokuk, Iowa, to the gold fields in Bannack City, Montana. It took considerable research to learn the lady's full name. She signed a letter sent back home with the diary, 'Kate,' but she always referred to her husband as just 'Mr. D.' It took some doing to find out that the 'D' stood for Dunlap.

"This was a great woman — you could tell it as you read the diary. We found out later that 'Mr. D.' was trained as a pharmacist, and had established a drug store in Bannack City. When Mr. Dunlap died leaving Kate with a young family, she assumed command and effectively ran the drug business. In addition, she was the midwife for the region.

"Most of this we learned later after months of research, but Kate's spirit showed through in the diary. I was impressed and Fred could see it. He asked if I wanted to edit the diary. I did. Years later it appeared as *The Montana Gold Rush Diary of Kate Dunlap,* beautifully designed as befitted the lady's dignity by E. Keith Eddington, with publication credits shared by Fred A. Rosenstocks' Old West Publishing Company and the University of Utah Press."

It was a part of Fred's philosophy that the quality of the physical book must equal the quality of the subject matter and the editing, and despite the fact that most of the Old West Publishing Company books were limited editions, they were, in themselves, superb works of art, with tasteful design, fine paper and binding, and highest quality printing. "Sometimes, to be helpful to the author, I would select a certain printer for two reasons: not only because I felt he was fine printer, but also because of his proximity to the author." A number of his author-editors — Robert Becker, Charles Camp, George Hammond, Dale Morgan — were associated with the University of California at Berkeley, and consequently when working with these people he would have the books printed by Lawton Kennedy of San Francisco, who, coincidentally, has the reputation of being the epitome of printers of fine books west of the Mississippi.

When Dale Morgan, who was perhaps one of the greatest scholar-authority-authors of Western history, was working on his first book for Old West Publishing Company (the *Overland Diary of James Avery Pritchard*), Fred had never met Lawton Kennedy. There had been some preliminary discussions between Kennedy and Morgan, and Fred came to San Francisco to meet the printer and finalize arrangements. "I had found some books published by Lawton Kennedy in Denver and talked to some people who knew him. I thought he would be too expensive, but the friends said he wouldn't be, so I made the trip. As I came into Kennedy's office I expected someone doing big projects only. I really felt like I had no business seeing him about such a small book. However, I was greeted warmly and began to discuss the details about the publication. Kennedy said he had heard of me. I told him I thought books of the kind I was publishing should not sell for more than fifteen dollars. Lawton Kennedy began to figure costs and other considerations, and said that he could do the job for that price. Right then and there I hired him."

That was the beginning of Fred's relationship with Lawton Kennedy, and since then they have done eight books together (to 1975). Each of these has won at least one prize for the workmanship in design, printing, and binding, as well as accolades for their contribution to the field of Western history.

As with the bookstore, Fred preferred the "old and rare," but he steadfastly maintained the textbook business for many years for financial reasons. Likewise, when the Old West Publishing Company began operating, he concentrated most heavily on the beautiful, significant journals and diaries that were, in themselves, collectors' items. But Fred invested large sums of money in these relatively limited editions, and seldom was there any financial gain. So it was partly through coincidence and partly through necessity that the Old West Publishing Company expanded into the textbook field.

"The dean of textbook salesmen in Colorado in the late thirties and forties," Harold Lindbloom, a onetime partner of Fred's in the schoolbook business relates, "was Fred Burkert who had worked for Ginn and Company since the 1890s and had come to Colorado to represent them shortly after the turn of the century. An entente of mutual respect between Burkert and his customers, and Fred and his customers developed into office space for Fred Burkert in the Bargain Book Store. Crowded as he was for book space, he allowed Burkert space even after the book salesman retired. He was eventually replaced by L. T. Sigstad, a native Minnesotan who had been something of a roving agent for Ginn and Company before transferring to Colorado.

"Sigstad, a former social studies teacher, had a keen interest in government, Western history, and geography. He liked what he saw and heard around Denver's Bargain Book Store. 'Sig,' as he was generally known by friends and customers, and the two Freds became fellow-admirers and co-workers. Sig, in his travels over Colorado and Wyoming, sensed a great need for curriculum materials dealing specifically with these sister states. Neither state had an up-to-date history, geography, or civics text . . . and this void was the subject of many discussions between Sigstad, Rosenstock, and their prospective customers."

The idea for such a text, designed for the seventh or eighth grade level, was talked over with Dr. LeRoy Hafen, the State Historian for Colorado at that time as well as an outstanding authority, scholar, and writer in the Western American history field. "A great deal of mutual interest and respect existed," says Lindbloom, "between Dr. Hafen and Rosenstock. It occurred to Fred that Dr. Hafen and his wife, Ann, would make a fine author team for a junior high school book." With considerable guidance in the early stages from Sigstad the book *Colorado: A Story of the State and Its People,* was completed by the Hafen team and published in 1943.

"We had great luck," Fred mentions, "in establishing that book as the official textbook all over the state. It was a terrific success. We must have sold something like 15,000 copies the first year. We continued to have one printing after another of that first edition until 1953; then we did a new edition with a slightly different title which continued through different printings until a complete revision with a new format was published in 1967." The current version, *Our State: Colorado,* was most recently printed in 1976.

Lindbloom points out that Rosenstock and Sigstad were innovators. "With an intuitive sense of pedagogical need, Teacher Resource Books were pioneered by these two men, for each of the texts covering Colorado and Wyoming (which came later) at both elementary and secondary levels. With the help of various authors and outstanding educators, these resource books were in tune with advanced educational thinking and encouraged teachers to go beyond the pages of the basic book — into films, filmstrips, recordings, individual and group projects — anything to encourage activity and enliven the pages of the correlated texts.

"Velma Linford, a vanguard Wyoming educator, authored *Wyoming: Frontier State* (1947), which was adopted as a textbook for the seventh, eighth and ninth grades. The Old West Publishing Company subsequently provided a text for grades three and four titled *Wyoming's People,* authored by Clarice Whittenburg. Likewise, Maude Frandsen developed a text for grades three and four in Colorado called *Our Colorado,* all of which were supplemented with teacher resource books." In an attempt to revive an interest in civics, Old West published *Colorado Citizen,* co-authored by Harold Lindbloom and Lawrence Sigstad, which included a study of Colorado's state constitution, a highlighted political history, an analysis of the checks and balances in all branches of government.

In later years, Velma Linford wrote, "I think it more than coincidence that the growth of interest in Western history coincides with Fred's venture in the book business. His Bargain Book Store was a mecca for Western historians and buffs. I sometimes sat up in his office (on the balcony) for hours and 'kibitzed' on conversations. From that lofty cubicle I persuaded Dr. Nolie Mumey to lend me his photograph plates for *Wyoming: Frontier State*. There Tom Ferril [noted Colorado poet, historian, and journalist] released his material for my use. There I looked through priceless bits of Americana — and there I argued historicity and historiography — school markets, textbook adoptions, Wyoming politics and education and every element of involvement in Western Americana because Fred Rosenstock was the person who knew or could find the elusive bits that made history come alive. Fred channeled my speechmaking into publications. He had an uncanny ability to bring together people and ideas."

Throughout Fred's career he demonstrated a rare combination of qualities: an unselfishness that enabled him to put aside his desire for personal gain whenever he felt that by so doing the interests of Western history would be better served, and a business acumen that enabled him to divert profits from one facet of his operation into another — the other generally being a project that would make a significant contribution to Western Americana.

This unselfishness is revealed in a small booklet, *Small Miracles in My Life as a Book Hunter* (designed and printed by Lawton and Alfred Kennedy — an appropriate touch) in which Fred writes of his obtaining a "terrific" item from William C. Smith in Cincinnati. "It was the manuscript private diary and personal color sketchbook of Lieutenant James W. Abert, of the Topographic Corps of the Army, whose special assignment, in 1846, was to make 'an examination of New Mexico' — soon after we had acquired the Territory. Abert, with his detail of men, started out on the Santa Fe Trail, became ill at Fort Bent, and while recuperating there made the famous authentic measurement, by feet and inches, of that old Fort. Today [1965], the National Park Service is reconstructing Fort Bent according to those miraculously survived Abert measurements. The Abert sketchbook, in particular, is a gem — many fine drawings in color, depicting towns, missions, Indians, and natural scenery.

"Finding this historical 'jewel' — the Abert diary and sketchbook — I regard as a small miracle; but here, too, was an exciting supplement. Years later, in altogether another part of the country — and in an entirely accidental manner (as if my friend Abert, in his celestial abode, was just leading me to it), I found the Government-published version, or report, of the Abert Narrative, with Abert's corrections and additions in his own hand, all through the volume!

"What happened to the Abert material? I had ideas of publishing it, but to publish, especially to reproduce the fine color sketches, would involve a greater outlay than I could afford; and I felt this deserved the utmost in reproduction and publication. My friend, Warren Howell, noted bookseller and publisher, of San Francisco, sold the Abert journal and accompanying material for me, to the noted collector, John Galvin." It was published by Howell under Galvin's auspices in 1966 under the title, *Western America in 1846–1847. The Original Travel Diary of Lieutenant J. W. Abert Who Mapped New Mexico for the United States Army, with Illustrations in Color from His Sketchbook.*

At times Fred would assume the role of an author's or publisher's representative — or a book wholesaler — if he found a book that was of particular interest to him. After reading Robert B. David's *Malcolm Campbell, Sheriff,* Fred commented that he "wrote what I think is the best, most objective account of the Johnson County Cattle War in Wyoming in the years 1891–92. Malcolm Campbell was actually only a minor character, and most of the book is a history of the Johnson County War." Fred was a close friend of David's foster parents, Edward David and his wife, and Ed would often visit the Rosenstock book store and regale Fred with virtual "eyewitness" accounts of the cattle wars. "He felt," Fred recalls, "that it was an exaggeration to say the big cattlemen hired fifty or sixty men called 'the invaders' who traveled at night en route from Texas. The idea was merely to scare a few of the rustlers. Of course, even the big cattlemen probably did a little rustling, with cattle wandering around in open country. The primary purpose of the 'war' was to scare out the little people — the big cattlemen didn't want any competition. They had a good thing going. They were 'cattle kings' and they labeled the interlopers as rustlers and set out to exterminate them."

The book had been published in Wyoming and had very limited distribution. Bob David was discouraged and talked to Fred about 'remaindering' his inventory, a method used by book publishers for disposing of excess books at very low prices. Fred was opposed to this suggestion and started to place the book in various retail outlets throughout the region. Today *Malcolm Campbell, Sheriff,* originally published in 1932, is a collector's item that sells for $20 to $25 a copy.

Fred developed such an interest in the cattle controversy following his involvement that he eventually published *Cow Country Cavalcade,* "a complete history of the cattle business in Wyoming from the early 1870s. It relates the trials and tribulations of the cattlemen, the 'fat' and 'lean' years; the cattle 'wars' and feuds; the 'barons' and the 'rustlers.' A fascinating authoritative account, embellished with many rare and unique illustrations," was the catalog description of the volume. It was written by Maurice Frink, a knowledgeable Western history scholar and the successor to LeRoy Hafen as Colorado State Historian.

The list of editors who worked with Fred Rosenstock on books for the Old West Publishing Company reads like a Who's Who in Western History, but perhaps the one figure towering above all the rest was Dale L. Morgan. This noted University of California (at Berkeley) historian edited *The West of William H. Ashley,* considered the classic of the American fur trade of the early Far West, and the winner of the New York Westerners' award as the outstanding book of Western history published in 1964. Just before Morgan's death in 1971 he had nearly completed *From Hudson Bay to the Great Salt Lake,* the journal of Joseph Burke in the Canadian and American West, 1843–1846. Burke, a botanist, had been "sent out from England in 1843 to collect plants and mammals for two great English collectors, voyaged to York Factory in the annual Hudson's Bay Company ship, and immediately traveled to Fort Edmonton with the year's brigade. After wintering on the Sas-

THE WEST OF
WILLIAM H. ASHLEY

The international struggle for the fur trade of the
Missouri, *the* Rocky Mountains, *and the* Columbia, *with explorations*
beyond the Continental Divide, *recorded in the diaries and letters*
of William H. Ashley *and his contemporaries*

1822-1838

Edited by Dale L. Morgan

Fred A. Rosenstock
THE OLD WEST PUBLISHING COMPANY
DENVER, COLORADO
1963

Brochure for The West of William H. Ashley

katchewan, he wandered during the summer of 1844 over the Peace River country before going on to the Columbia. From Walla Walla he set out for Fort Hall on the Snake River, and made that his headquarters over the next two years, while with Hudson's Bay parties he roamed northern Utah, eastern Idaho, and western Montana. In the fall of 1846 Burke rode back to the Columbia with Jesse Applegate, traveling the newly opened Applegate Cutoff. Burke's letters to his patrons, amounting to a daily journal, are our only year-round record of life at Fort Hall during the Hudson's Bay Company epoch. He describes the conduct of the fur trade, touchy relations with Utes, Snakes, Nez Perces and other tribes, and much more, scarcely known to historians till now."

The complete list of Old West Publishing Company titles to date (for more books are in process) may well represent one of the most extensive collections of rare Western Americana published in the last thirty-five years.* And it was Fred's knowledge of the old West, his ability to ferret out the dusty journals and diaries and maps and to spend years, if necessary, to find the perfect editor for a particular project that made it all possible.

In *The West of William H. Ashley,* Morgan (in a special note) remarks on his relationship with his publisher, another indication of the unusual character of the Old West Publishing Company: "Fred A. Rosenstock has been my friend nearly from the commencement of my interest in Ashley, and we agreed almost ten years ago that he should be the publisher. Patiently he has waited all this time without pressuring me for manuscript, nor has he been appalled by its final bulk. We were agreed that Lawton R. Kennedy must print the book, confident that Lawton, his wife Freda, and their son Alfred, distinguished San Francisco printers as well as our warm friends, would dress William H. Ashley as he warrants."

One must wonder how the void in Western history represented by publication of this rare material would have been filled had there not been an Old West Publishing Company.

*See Appendix for a list and description of major titles of Old West Publishing Company.

CHAPTER XIII

A NEW WORLD OF BOOKS

ONE OF THE TYPICAL TRAGEDIES of the pioneer and mining towns of the Old West was the virtual certainty that a major fire would occur, frequently destroying the entire business district and often so ravaging the place that it became an instant ghost town. So well acquainted with Western Americana was Fred that reading about such conflagrations was a matter of historical interest, but little more.

But following the night of November 30, 1949, when fire struck the Bargain Book Store, he had firsthand knowledge of the frightful consequences of flames razing a building. The physical structure could be replaced, but the rare volumes that were damaged or destroyed were gone forever. Fortunately, the fire happened before he had accumulated his greatest collection of Russell paintings, and before he had completely converted his operation into the comprehensive library of Western Americana that it would eventually become.

Perhaps the 1949 fire was another miracle, at least the catalyst that precipitated his eventual decision to move to a new location. The rare book room (which he had built following the fire) became the center of Fred's attention, and he and Frances began to discuss more and more the possibility of disposing of the Bargain Book Store with its emphasis on school and technical books, and creating a new business concentrating solely on rare volumes, first editions, Western Americana, and Western art.

Their daughter, Marilyn, made her feelings known, and this may have added impetus to their ultimate decision. According to Marilyn,

the schoolbook business was the greatest competitor for her parents'
time. "People didn't realize," she said, "that every summer the whole
store had to be practically revamped to accommodate the upcoming
schoolbook season — and this went on until Christmas." It was the pres-
sure of this aspect of the business, she feels, that contributed to the deterioration of her mother's health.

She would write notes frequently, when she was ten or eleven, concerning the Bargain Book Store, and ask her father to sign them. One
such "document" read: "I *promise* [underlined three times] that when
I sell the Bargain Book Store I will come home at 6:00 [the word 'approximately' is added in Fred's handwriting] and *stay home* [under-
lined three times]. Signed, Fred A. Rosenstock. Witnessed by F. A.
Burkert, Marilyn Rosenstock, Frances Rosenstock." Perhaps the key
phrase was "when I sell," for Marilyn relates that "it was ironic, in a
way, for by the time he sold the Bargain Book Store I had long since
left."

By the late fifties, both Fred's interest and energies were devoted
more and more to obtaining and selling collections, rare books and original editions relating to Western Americana, and there was more and
more conversation about a new store and a complete abandonment of
the general and textbook operation. He had by this time developed a
solid reputation as a leading bookman of the West. On May 31, 1955,
Robert L. Perkin wrote a feature story in the *Rocky Mountain News:*
"Who is Denver's best-known bookman? If you asked that question in
Glen Dawson's shop in Los Angeles, at Peter Decker's in New York
City, John Howell's in San Francisco, or in any other of the famous
bookshops of America, you'd get the same answer: Fred Rosenstock."

The article provides some interesting insights. Perkin quotes Fred
saying, "I just enjoy seeing and touching books. It's still there — the
same old thrill as in the beginning. It keeps me youthful, and that's
necessary in this business. And I'd say a love of books is an axiom for
keeping young. Describing books and searching for them breathes more
interest into the life of a true bookman than anything else — even the

owning of books you seek out." This is the life philosophy of a true bookman.

His friends and family, including Marilyn, continued to prod him concerning the new store. On February 13, 1960, a letter from Dale Morgan chided Fred because he had not yet taken the step: "We begin to be skeptical about you, Fred; it looks like you just cannot bring yourself to sacrifice your retail book property."

Nevertheless, by the end of 1960 he had taken some positive steps. If it were just a move to a new location, the problem of transporting the inventory would be difficult; but the logistics became far more complex when it involved disposing of a major part of his business on the one hand, and adding to his collection of rare Western Americana on the other. During 1961 he began to reduce his inventory of textbooks and general books — a step that proved to be a windfall for the recipients. Lyman Tyler, acting as an intermediary, arranged for Brigham Young University to check the holdings of their library against the 75,000 general books in Fred's stock, covering general literature and criticism, fiction, poetry, plays, theater, music, art, essays, journalism, general history, biography, description and travel, natural history, economics, sociology, politics and government, psychology, philosophy, logic and ethics, Christian and eastern religions, and occult literature.

The University was allowed to purchase these books at an average of one dollar a copy. Over a period of three years a rented truck, driven by members of the library staff, would periodically make the trip from Provo, Utah, to Denver, load up with books and head back to Provo.

Textbooks, technical books, and what was still an imposing stock of general books, along with the fixtures, goodwill and a going business were sold to Johnny Johnsen, president of the Nebraska Book Company, operators of a chain of college book stores in the mountain and midwest states.

Between the various complications of moving to a new store, disposing of the old stock and searching for additional collections, while continuing to operate the Bargain Book Store, placed considerable pressures on Fred. In Fred's terminology, another miracle occurred. K. K. Damon, a young, thirty-six-year-old rancher from Nebraska with a deep interest in books, decided to give up his interest in the Lone Star Ranch and entered into a limited partnership with the Rosenstocks.

Fred would ponder the question of which books and collections he wished to move to the new store, then he and Damon would decide where the volumes should go and the enthusiastic ex-rancher would build the shelves, supervise the moving of the books and arrange them in the new store. Some of the decisions were difficult, but others were easy. All of the Western Americana would, of course, be moved. His collections of the United States Geological Survey and Bureau of American Ethnology were considered one of the best — if not the best — in the country, and they would go to the new location. Other volumes had to be considered on a book-to-book basis, such as his special collections of general history and selected scholarly works and his extensive collection of art books.

Before the move was completed another opportunity came Damon's way, but he stayed with the Rosenstocks until the move was complete, for which Fred was tremendously grateful. "Without Damon, life at that point would have been much more difficult."

By the summer of 1962 the shelving was complete and the remaining inventory had been transferred. Lyman Tyler, with his expertise in book classification, his knowledge of the Western history field, and his close personal relationship with Fred, was the logical person to work with the Rosenstocks in arranging the new store. On the right hand side of the wide aisle were three classifications of books: hunting, gun books, and ecology (natural history); railroads and transportation; Western art books. Fine bindings, both individual volumes and sets, were shelved along the back of the display room.

But the great collections — the fabulous library of Rosenstock Western Americana — extended the entire length of the left-hand side of the store. In all, seventeen classifications were represented: General books about the West; new and current western books; the Colorado collection; the collection on California, Nevada, and Hawaii; Fur trade and exploration; the American Indian; the army in the West, outlaws, frontier justice; the Texas collection; cowboys, cattle, and life on the range; Arizona and New Mexico; the Northwest — Washington, Oregon, Alaska, Idaho, Montana; Wyoming, the Dakotas, Nebraska, Kansas; Western literature and poetry; Utah and the Mormons; Western biographies; Mexico and Latin America; the collection on the Civil War.

The formal opening of "Fred A. Rosenstock, Books," perhaps the most significant rare book dealer between Chicago and San Francisco, was coincidentally (Fred would say, "miraculously") during the time of the organizational meeting of what was to become the Western History Association. A year before in Santa Fe a preliminary conference was held to discuss plans for a formal history organization, and such a formalization occurred at the October, 1962, meeting in Denver.

Whether coincidence or miracle or a brilliantly thought-out arrangement, it was perfect timing. As early as April of 1962 Fred and Robert Athearn, historian from the University of Colorado and one of the WHA organizers, discussed plans for a cocktail party for those attending the inaugural meeting of this prestigious association.

However, as summer waned the prospects for a grand opening by October dimmed. Lyman Tyler took up temporary residence in Denver and enlisted the aid of several rather notable personages (and friends of Fred) to undertake a crash program to get the store ready. Tyler was given twenty-four-hour access to the new store and he and his volunteers worked around the clock. Dr. Nolie Mumey, surgeon, author, collector, charter member of the Denver Westerners, constructed a specially designed wheeled book truck (made of oak) at his home workshop. Lawrence Sigstad, the sales representative for Ginn and Company and Fred's partner in the schoolbook publishing business, and his son devoted many midnight hours to the project, along with a half-dozen or more professional people who willingly donned overalls and jeans to help a friend.

The battle was won, and the grand opening cocktail party was listed under "Highlights" for Thursday, October 11, four to six P.M., in the

WHA program. Fred arranged for shuttle buses to take members from the downtown hotel to the new store (located on East Colfax Avenue, some fifteen blocks from the business district), and then back to the hotel. Fred assumed that it would be a typical open house, with people browsing through, sipping a cocktail, and leaving. Actually, virtually no one left. They came and they stayed, until approximately four hundred people filled the store. The crowd thinned by eight o'clock when the WHA evening sessions started, but many stayed on until almost midnight, deciding to forego the Thursday night WHA meeting.

In addition to the formal announcement, Lawton Kennedy published a reprint of an early Colorado newspaper which was handed out to the guests as a keepsake.

The opening of the store was a major event in the rare booksellers' arena, and hundreds of telegrams and congratulatory letters poured in from every section of the country. Charles K. Stotlemeyer, a Maryland bookseller, wrote, "It must be a great satisfaction to have such a fine shop . . . and also, a great responsibility." Al Friedman, who had worked at the bookstore as a student, said, "I know that it will be a financial success, with you at the helm; but far more important, it is and will be accomplishing a most important function in man's struggle to know and retain his past. You are serving mankind and his culture in a most unique way . . ."

And Dale Morgan, too busy on the Ashley project to attend, wrote: "Lawton [Kennedy] has told me that your new place is simply out of this world, and with the resounding send-off it got at the time of the [Western History Association] Conference last month, I am sure it will be *the* place of rendezvous for bibliophiles in the western half of the continent. I express my pleasure and satisfaction all over again, that you have been able to bring about this mighty change and begin to live your life along the pattern you have dreamed for years (with no blue books or catechisms)."

The first few months — October, November, December — were busy ones at Fred Rosenstock, Books, with numerous author-autograph

The opening of "Fred A. Rosenstock, Books"

parties, hundreds of friends and curiosity-seekers dropping in, and a flurry of Christmas buyers. But in January the full impact of the different nature of the business, and the move from a busy downtown location to an outlying section, had a disturbing effect on Fred. The store was no longer filled with people, and the character of his customers as well as the entire atmosphere changed.

Gradually the business through the mail increased, as well as the number of persons on the mailing list. Authors, librarians, collectors from all over the world began to pay visits to the store, spending hours or days becoming familiar with this vast repertoire of Western Americana. Other dealers from distant cities were frequent buyers of some of his rare, choice volumes. At times librarians and collectors would bring cameras with them and shoot the title pages of hundreds of books so that they could check them against their own holdings upon returning home, later to order those books they did not have.

Although the collection of books on the shelves in the display room was impressive, Fred's entire library was far more extensive, with thousands of volumes in the storeroom at the back of the store, and thousands more in the Rosenstock private collection at his home. Only a few of the collectors or serious scholars were invited to see these volumes.

The Rosenstock residence was in effect a "house of books." Most accessible for ready reference were a few hundred volumes in the living room, and the largest collection was located in the library downstairs. But there were loaded bookshelves in the two basement bedrooms and in the closet under the stairs, with the bibliography collection in the hall. One room was seldom mentioned and seldom included on the tour. It was the collection in the "fruit room" and being taken to this favored spot was not unlike being invited to see the crown jewels.

Most Western historians — whether scholars, writers, or buffs — concede that two occurrences in the past half-century did much to make Denver one of the major centers of reference materials on the old West. One was the opening of the Western History Department of the Denver Public Library in 1934, and the other was the opening of Fred Rosenstock, Books. From the day in 1920 when he left the train at Denver's Union Station to purchase a new pair of glasses, his love of the Mile-High City was second only to his affection for his wife and his love of rare books. Therefore, Fred was an eager supporter of Denver, and particularly if a library was involved. In the early twenties, he had a close personal relationship with Chalmers Hadley, the city librarian, and later with Dr. Malcolm G. Wyer, who served as Chief Librarian of the Denver Public Library for more than a quarter of a century. In a brochure on the Western History Department published in 1965 special tribute was paid to Fred Rosenstock "for the deep interest he has shown in strengthening our collection."

Alys H. Freeze, who became the head of the Western History Department in 1957, wrote shortly before her retirement, "In thinking over the years that the Western History Department has been collecting material — published, manuscript and pictorial — I am increasingly impressed with the amount that has been secured through the efforts of Fred Rosenstock. . . . Few institutions in this area have been able to afford to hire scouts to locate materials for purchase or gifts to enlarge the scope of their special collections. So they are dependent upon knowledgeable book dealers to do this. Fred's serendipity and memory have enabled him to provide either the book or knowledge of its location and provenance in an amazing number of instances. Rarely has he handled a book he has forgotten.

"His book stock in the field of Western Americana has been by far the most important source for the libraries and private collectors in the region. Had he not located here it would have been a severe loss to Denver and the Rocky Mountain area.

"Never have I entered his store but that some facet of history has become more vivid because of his knowledge of historical events. Each item is a part of his being. He is a gentle man with a slight old world courtesy. . . . A great void will exist when he is no longer in the book business."

He not only provided help, guidance, counsel, and materials to the

Denver Public Library, but was an important force in the development of the library at Brigham Young University from a relatively small collection of books to its position today as one of the foremost university libraries in the field of Western history. Lyman Tyler, who became the Director of Libraries for BYU in 1954, writes of his relationship with the Rosenstocks: "The role that Fred and Frances played in giving assistance to me as the librarian during a period that saw the library holdings more than triple in size . . . is truly admirable." Tyler cites a typical example of how valuable a bookman — particularly with the acumen of a Fred Rosenstock — can be to a library, in this case reference is made to the collection of works by and about Herman Melville. Fred Rosenstock learned of Dr. Tyrus Hillway, a professor at Colorado State College and the founder of the Melville Society, and became particularly interested in the material Dr. Hillway had collected. He had gathered books, Tyler notes, "not only related to Melville, but background books about whales and whaling, and about the lives of the sailors as well as the ships they sailed in. . . .

"Tyrus Hillway lived for a time at New London, Connecticut, second largest whaling port in the United States, and there developed his interest in whales, whaling, and Melville-related topics. So extensive was his knowledge that he acted as a consultant during the filming of the movie version of Melville's *Moby Dick*."

Fred eventually obtained the collection and later sold it to Brigham Young University, including not only the different issues of Melville first editions, but subsequent editions, as well as books about the author, his times, and the people about whom he wrote. "Historians and literary scholars are thus provided with an opportunity to study one of the greatest writers of life at sea, as well as obtaining a greater insight — through availability of extensive background material — into his character and Melville's obsession: the universal conflict between good and evil." Fred was unquestionably an astute businessman, but he had a philanthropic spirit in his dealings with schools and universities. The early issue of the first American edition of *Moby Dick* alone was valued at $225 at that time (1962), yet he sold the University the entire collection at an average cost of less than five dollars a volume.

A few of the many important collections obtained by Brigham Young University included an unusually rich treasure of fourteen hundred volumes of state, county, and local histories; an important collection containing several thousand photographs of the middle west and the mountain west covering half a century; a substantial array of books on the history of the English and American theatre including representative plays, "prompt" copies, playbills, biographies of actors and actresses, and histories of important theatres and theatrical groups; the Edwin L. Sabin collection on Kit Carson; and the James P. Beckwourth Collection. This latter material was acquired by Fred through his contact with Howard Crocker, a professional golfer and Denver pharmacist who from time to time brought items to Fred that had belonged to F. B. Crocker, Howard's grandfather and a pioneer businessman of Denver. One day Fred was invited to the Crocker home to look at some of the old records the family had accumulated. Among them Fred discovered account books and manuscripts that had belonged to the famous mountain man, Jim Beckwourth, who had made his home in Denver from 1859 to 1865. There was some correspondence, letters from the Vasquez brothers and Jim Bridger, and Beckwourth's will dated 1864.

When Tyler resigned as librarian at Brigham Young University to join the faculty at the University of Utah, "the library (at Utah) was allowed to select over $100,000 worth of choice Western Americana from the Rosenstock's personal collection and from their stock at the store." Likewise the libraries at the University of Arizona at Tucson, the University of Wyoming at Laramie and Princeton University have all been enriched through their relationship with the Rosenstocks. The Mormon *Book of Commandments,* which Fred obtained on his trip West with his daughter, was eventually acquired by the Bancroft Library (University of California at Berkeley).

As in the circumstances surrounding Fred's purchase of the *Book of Commandments,* the buying of rare books can be a risky venture, not only with the risk of obtaining an imperfect copy, but also the risk that the particular book — for a variety of reasons — will not sell, at least at the price the dealer paid for it. The *Book of Commandments* was, in fact, a valuable item, but Fred's return on his investment, considering his apprehension, was only nominal, receiving ultimately $2,300 for the volume after paying $1,900.

Peter Decker, a most reliable and knowledgeable dealer, sold Fred an original German edition of Maximilian's *Travels in the Interior of North America,* "with all the eighty-one plates in immaculate, highly colored condition." The final price was $2,000, and Fred had waited for its arrival with anxiety. "I looked at the plates rather hurriedly," he wrote to Decker, "saw some things which I wasn't exactly happy about, then thought that before writing you I would first look over the set at the Denver Public Library, also the set in the Denver Art Museum. Briefly, these are the things that stand out: This appears to be a 'made-up' set from various issues and periods of publication. . . . In the set that the Denver Library owns, every plate is uniform, the same kind of paper and every plate has the stamped or 'pressed' imprint of Bodmer on it. On the set you sent me, only about a third of the plates have the Bodmer pressed imprints. . . . Several prints in my set look real new, so new, in fact, that I confess I am a bit worried. I have noted the description of the Maximilian in the last Wagner-Camp, and I note the reference to the 1922 reprint edition done in England. I am just wondering if the 'real new-looking ones' could possibly have been of this 1922 reprint vintage?"

Peter Decker was able to reassure Fred and explain the difference in the plates. In referring to the 1922 edition, he wrote that "there was no edition published in England in 1922. There was, however, a small edition of the plates run off by the then present head of the Wied family in Leipzig in 1922. The plates were uncolored. This Leipzig edition is rarer than the original edition. Miss Quigley of the Montclair Public Library, a Bodmer authority, states that she can't locate but two copies in America of this edition and both are incomplete.

". . . The main thing to notice in the Max, which is not going to get any cheaper, is: Are the plates all present? Are they highly colored and suitable for framing? If so, you have a set of the Max. . . . As a final summary, I would say that your set was made-up, but it was sold at a price approximately a little less than a third of the current retail value and I can't see any hope of this great pictorial record depreciating. . . . I have handled during the past fifteen years at least twelve copies of the Max, all of them different. I hope this sufficiently explains my attitude. I am sure that you have not bought a pig in a poke and that some day you will thank me."

Fred was not only satisfied, but felt he had added much to his education concerning Maximilian. Over the years he purchased and sold more copies. In the late sixties he sold a black and white set for $7,000, and a colored set about 1970 for $12,000.

This was one facet of Fred's life, being fully engrossed in a discussion concerning the technical points of "the Max" or the *Book of Commandments*. But there were other facets — such as his desire to be a physical part of this Great West that he had adopted as his own. His deep involvement with the Westerners was fostered by his desire to become as much a part of the West as possible.

One of his fellow Westerners, Dabney Otis Collins, collector, writer, history buff, recalls that "the human side of this man of many gifts came out strongly in the old-time Wyoming ranch tours sponsored by the Albany County Historical Society. I was with Fred and Frances on three of these tours. The long cavalcade of cars started at the Laramie (Wyoming) courthouse. Frances did the driving. Between head-hung naps — complete sleep, deep and dreamless, in a second — Fred absorbed the immensity of land and sky, colored it in broad strokes of historical background. In conversation with such authorities as University of Wyoming's Dr. Robert Burns and Dr. Al Larson, with old-time Swan Land and Cattle Company cowboy Bud Gillespie, Fred Hesse of the famed 76 Ranch, and historian Velma Linford, his questions were as perceptive as his interest genuine.

"One of the trail tours took us to four assassination sites of Tom

Horn, killer said to be hired by a group of cattlemen to rid the range of rustlers. Visiting the bunkhouse where Tom Horn slept between murder assignments, seeing the nail in the bedpost which he used in braiding horsehair belts and bridles (a hobby of Horn's), Fred was a million miles from his storeful of books. I have a picture of the two of us beside the boulder behind which Horn shot his last victim, the boy Willie Nickell.

"An intellectual of the highest order, successful businessman and art dealer, yet Fred Rosenstock had never lost his intimate touch with his fellow man."

CHAPTER XIV

FROM BOOKS TO ART

BOOK COLLECTORS — particularly those whose interest centered on Western Americana — were much aware of the value of the illustrations, which often were more valuable than the text itself. The Bodmer plates, the Ferris map, the Mathews sketches of Colorado, the line drawings in *Harper's Weekly* — all were significant and valuable contributions to an understanding of the American frontier.

During the 1920s, in Fred Rosenstock's early days as a rare book dealer, he frequently bought and sold books with beautiful illustrations by numerous Western artists, including Charles Russell, Frederic Remington, Howard Pyle, and N. C. Wyeth. Between his inquisitive nature and his thirst for knowledge, Fred began to contact experts in the field of art, learning much about the lives of the painters of the West, as well as techniques, the fine points to look for in their work, not unlike the procedure he used in analyzing a fine first edition.

By the time Russell died in 1926, Fred had studied many of his paintings thoroughly. He had learned to observe the background, to study the stance and the expression of movement in the horse, the faces of the cowboys or the Indians. The more he learned of the man and his paintings, the more convinced he was that Russell was one of the foremost of Western artists. In these early years, the desire to own some original paintings was not unlike a boy's dream of owning a Flexible Flyer — and just as unobtainable. But the itch was there.

While making one of his trips East, Fred became acquainted with Merle Johnson, an authority on American first editions. He also had about a hundred drawings and sketches by Frederic Remington. The young bookman looked at them longingly, and finally asked Johnson if he would consider selling any of these originals. "Someday, perhaps," was Johnson's reply. Fred was thwarted in his desire to own these particular originals, but he mentioned the collection to Malcolm Wyer, and the Denver Public Library ultimately obtained Johnson's Remington collection for their Western History Department.

In the depths of the depression, Fred — convinced of the greatness of Russell's work — realized that this would be a good time to acquire Russell paintings. But these were hard years for the Rosenstocks, and a small watercolor by Russell would cost about $250 to $300. Usually, after the fall schoolbook sale, they had a little extra money and Fred decided to invest it in Russells.

His first few purchases were watercolors, but eventually — as the result of advertising in Montana newspapers — he had an opportunity to buy an oil for a thousand dollars. After a bit of soul-searching and long discussions with Frances, he made the purchase. The painting, *Indian Fight,* would be valued between $40,000 and $50,000 in 1975.

He continued advertising, and began receiving more offers. A lawyer in Butte advised him that he was closing an estate and had two Russells for sale, one about fifteen by twenty inches and the other sixteen by twenty-two. Under the terms of the will they had to be sold together. The lawyer was asking $500 for the pair. Fred expressed interest and requested photographs. One, which he described as "a typical scene of a cowboy on a bucking bronco, hanging on by a thread, like he would fall off the next second," he liked very much.

The other painting, Fred felt, was a poor one. Charlie Russell, so the stories go, liked his liquor and had been known to dash off a painting in a hurry and trade it to Sid Willis at the Mint Saloon in Great Falls for drinks. (Eventually the Mint had forty or fifty Russells which were later acquired by the Amon Carter Museum.) Fred concluded that the second painting was one the great artist had traded for booze.

The scene was of a herd of cattle on the Montana range after a long, tough winter. "They were huddled in one corner of the corral because of the cold," Fred describes, "and they looked to be nothing but skin and bones. There was snow on the ground, and outside the corral were other animals — all you could see were their eyes. On the opposite side of the corral was the bull, by himself. He seemed to be misshapen and humpy — a skin-covered skeleton." Fred was concerned and asked for other opinions, which corroborated his feeling that it wasn't a good painting. He attempted to buy the one painting, and was turned down, though the lawyer agreed to sell both for $450. He sought out other so-called experts, and again they confirmed his feeling that the second painting was inferior. For weeks he thought about the two Russells, and finally decided that he would not change his mind.

Several years later, Frank Dobie was visiting at the Rosenstock home and the conversation eventually swung around to Russells. Dobie had a few, mostly from the 1890–1900 period, and Fred asked which — of the Russell paintings he owned — he liked best. Dobie said, "It is a cold, winter scene. The cattle are in a corral — cows on one side and the bull on the other. The eyes of a couple of wolves can be seen shining out of the darkness. The cattle are emaciated. It's really a masterpiece." Fred smiled grimly and asked Dobie about the circumstances. Dobie confirmed that he had bought it in the mid-thirties from an estate, and that he had to buy the two paintings as a set. Fred stifled a tinge of bitterness, obtaining some consolation from the fact that it was Dobie who bought it. Today the painting is considered one of the prime Russells.

It was Homer Britzman who, more than any other individual, made a serious Russell collector out of Fred Rosenstock. Britzman had graduated from the University of Colorado and after World War I began to scout oil fields for one of the major producers. "He had," Fred recalls, "a nose for oil. He worked mostly in Wyoming and Montana, eventually becoming a partner in one of the companies.

"Once while scouting for oil in Montana, after a lot of hard riding, he came to this little one-horse town with one small hotel where he put up for the night. It was late and the old man at the desk was half asleep.

Britzman noticed a painting on the wall with a cowboy on a horse riding over the Montana terrain. He became interested in the painting and
noticed the name of the artist, Charles Russell, and remarked about it.
This brought the old man to life. He began to talk about his state's
greatest artist. He asked Britzman to find the 'rabbit' in the picture.
Britzman scrutinized it more closely and said, 'I can't see any rabbit.'
The old man pointed his finger at one portion of the painting and, lo
and behold, there was a rabbit. This little incident marked the start of
Britzman's interest in Russell.

"As Britzman traveled in Montana after that he kept his eyes open
for Russells, and bought some quite reasonably. About this time — 1925
— Nancy Russell was having difficulty with the harsh Montana climate
and she and Charlie decided to build a home in Pasadena. Charlie Russell died in Great Falls before it was completed, but his widow saw it
through to completion and lived there from 1926 to her death in 1939.

"At the time she died Britzman was already known as one of the
most active collectors of Russell. He knew about and had his eye on the
collection at Trails End. The executor of the estate decided to sell the
paintings and the home at auction. Britzman knew there would be competition; somehow he learned that C. R. Smith, president of American
Air Lines, would be one of the bidders. Before the sale the two men
agreed to make a combined purchase rather than fight each other. They
flipped a coin to see who got the first choice. Smith had the number one
selection, Britzman the second, and so on. Between them they must have
acquired seventy-five to one hundred paintings, plus the Russell correspondence and the home. Britzman obtained Trail's End, the letters,
many clay models of bronzes which had never been cast, numerous other
artifacts and personal mementos of the Russells."

Britzman started the Trail's End Publishing Company and became
quite active as a Western history buff, being named the first sheriff of the
Los Angeles Posse of The Westerners. About 1949 Britzman came to
Colorado to attend a meeting of the Denver Westerners and to sell
Trail's End books to Denver booksellers. Fred became not only one of

his best customers but also a good friend. From time to time Britzman would sell Fred a Russell, and at one time they made a trade — two Britzman Russells for one Rosenstock watercolor depicting an Indian woman mourning over her dead baby, something Britzman wanted very badly.

"Britzman developed a yen for the artist Nicolai Fechin, who had come to the Southwest in the late 1920s and started painting Southwest scenes. His style was altogether different from Russell, and Britzman was always ready to sell a Russell to get money to buy a Fechin."

On the trip to California with Marilyn in 1951, Fred purchased about half of Britzman's library on Western art and the West in general for around $35,000. A fair value at the time, this price in 1976 would be considered a steal.

"When Homer Britzman died his affairs were in a chaotic condition. His wife, Helen, had been living at Palmer Lake, Colorado, taking care of some of their property. When he became ill she returned to Pasadena. After the estate was settled, she put the entire Russell collection up for sale. Because she regarded me as a friend, she gave me first chance. This was about 1955 and Russell values were still nowhere near what they later became. There were approximately thirty to thirty-five Russells, and she put a price of $120,000 on the collection — just the paintings, not the correspondence or other items."

Fred had about $50,000 available, but would need to borrow $70,000. His bank had no experience in loaning money for buying paintings, and none of the directors knew anything about Charlie Russell. Fred had to explain Russell's reputation as a Western artist, the value of the paintings and their salability. After three meetings and almost a month later, the directors told Fred he could have the money, *without* security, but with the stipulation that they would be allowed to display the collection in the rotunda of the bank for thirty days.

Fred called Helen Britzman to tell her he had the money. "She said she had had a nervous breakdown," Fred relates, "and was going to a hospital. She asked me not to press her then. A month went by. I was

impatient, of course, but I didn't bother her. Finally, when I called —
she had returned home from the hospital — she said she had mulled
over the price she had made me and decided it was too low. She thought
it ought to be $140,000. I had made definite arrangements with the bank
and didn't want to go back for another $20,000. I told her I had gone as
far as I could. She then sold the collection to the Hammer Gallery of
New York for at least $140,000, possibly more. I knew I had made a
mistake by not buying the Russells when I had the opportunity, in spite
of what seemed an unfair advance in price after I'd been given a firm
offer."

Fred expressed his deep interest in Russell in a booklet prepared for
a Western art exhibit in 1970: "As a boy in Rochester, I was avidly con-
suming all sorts of reading matter on the so-called Wild West, including
the dime novels of that day. It was natural to fall under the spell of the
Western illustrators as well. I came to know and to be charmed by the
work of Russell and other artists who painted the West 'as she was.' It
seemed to me even then that, far beyond technical pictorial representation, Russell put something indefinable in his pictures that made them
vibrant, more true to life, something expressing almost a philosophy of
the cowboy and the Indian, the spirit and atmosphere of the Old West,
such as perhaps no other artist approached or understood.

"I learned that Russell also wrote about as well as painted the Old
West. I devoured his stories, which had a flavor of authenticity and a
sense of humor I had not encountered previously in any other artist or
writer. I began to want to know more about Russell, to learn about his
life, and to discover what made him so different. I learned about his being a cowboy himself; how he left his comfortable St. Louis home as a
boy and hired out to a cattleman in Montana; how he began to paint
during chow time on the range; and how he developed his ability without benefit of an art lesson. Also, I came to know about Russell's great
feeling for the Indian as the real first American, and about his love and
portrayal of the cowboy, the horse, the grass, and the terrain of his be-
loved Montana.

"Russell passed away in 1926. I was saddened by this as I had entertained a hope that I might meet him personally. The hard times of the depression had set in, and it was all my wife and I could do to keep on an even keel in our struggling bookstore. However, the fire engendered by our enthusiasm for Russell could not be stilled. With meager funds that might have been more economically applied to more practical uses, we managed somehow to find the funds to buy an occasional Russell painting. . . . Altogether, as I reflect on it now, my 'falling in love' with Russell has added spice to life and has been an inspiring and rewarding lifelong experience."

By the time he had moved into the new store in 1962, Fred had accumulated, in addition to his Russells, some Remingtons, two Morans, a few Harvey Youngs and some fine Boreins as well as the works of several other regional artists. He was also collecting the paintings and photography of William H. Jackson, and became acquainted with Jackson's son, Clarence, who at that time (1946) was completing arrangements with Scribner's for publication of a book about his father, *Picture Maker of the Old West*. He had an extensive collection of paintings, photographs, and ephemera that he had inherited, a good portion of which Fred eventually acquired.

At one period in his life, Clarence had been partially supporting himself by making light photos of his father's pictures, then retouching them. Fred was impressed by the work, and suggested that a set of Jackson photographs be made up, and retouched by Clarence. He did an initial group of fifty or sixty photographs, and later made five or six additional sets. For the Rosenstocks, Clarence had the pictures beautifully mounted and bound in three full-leather volumes.

Originally it was planned that the Rosenstock paintings would be displayed at the store as a Western decorator motif, but would not be offered for sale. The collecting of art was started primarily as a hobby, a personal means of becoming more fully married to the romantic Old West. But within two or three years, Fred had quietly and without fanfare become a dealer in art. "Once you begin to display paintings, people come in for books, see the paintings and inquire about them. It doesn't take very long to develop a clientele. It all comes from building up your collection and having something to show. . . . It was the same with art as it had been with the specialty book collectors in the old days. People became imbued with the idea that I was building something. Newspaper reporters began to call and were so impressed that they wrote us up as a gallery.

"As I became more active in acquiring Western art and artifacts, I would take trips to see what other dealers had, into New Mexico, Arizona, and California. My customers and friends knew that when I took a trip I would usually bring back special books and art. . . . It eventually got to be known over the country that Fred Rosenstock had a gallery of early Western artists."

Fred took a certain pride in making art collectors out of his book buyers, convinced that this added dimension was necessary for a complete understanding of Western history. For the same reason, with the help of Major Gehman, L. D. "Drew" Bax, and Norman Feder, he began to acquire Indian artifacts — pottery, basketry, and leather work, in addition to Navajo rugs.

Although he usually had several hundred paintings on display at the store, virtually all of his Russell collection and other fine works were not offered for sale and were kept at his home.

Toward the end of the sixties Fred's reputation as an art collector and dealer was, at the least, nationwide. James Parsons, friend and art connoisseur, discussed with Fred the possibility of an exhibition, to give the general public an opportunity to see for the first time the many great paintings currently housed in his residence. On November 28, 1969, the exhibition, "One Hundred Years of Western Art," opened with a reception for selected clientele, and continued until December 24. An attractive catalog was issued, and a total of 352 paintings were included with an accumulative value (at that time) of $354,000. The artists truly represented practically all of the most famous Western painters of the past century: Albert Bierstadt, Ed Borein, Maynard Dixon, Nick Eggen-

Self Portrait #1, *watercolor by Charles M. Russell*
Courtesy Harry A. Lockwood, Cincinnati, Ohio, and Sotheby Parke Bernet, Inc.

hofer, Peter Hurd, W. H. D. Koerner, Frank Tenney Johnson, Thomas Moran, Charles Schreyvogel, and dozens of others, including of course Russell and Remington.

Parsons, in his introduction to the catalog, wrote that "long before Western paintings became popular and in good demand, artists and dealers sold to isolated collectors who made purchases based on their personal instinctive feeling of value and worth, and an inherent love of fine art.

"Fred Rosenstock was and is one of these collectors. True, his business has been rare books and Western Americana, and books are his first love. But he has also been a collector of art for forty years, and his place of business has been a crossroads for artists and writers, dealers and professional people from across the country. Had you been a regular visitor at Fred's book shop over the years you might have met and talked with J. Frank Dobie, Frank Waters, Harold McCracken, Robert Lindneux, Raphael Lillywhite, Fred Renner (the Russell authority) or any of a hundred other notables in the Western art, books, museum, and gallery field.

"Long ago no less a painter than Albert Bierstadt commented that art and books were natural companions and that libraries everywhere should expose the public to good art as well as good writing. Fred, for an individual, has done this on an impressive scale.

"Thus it is fitting that our show, organized as a tribute to those who painted and loved the West, should be held at Fred's place of business in the company of books, pamphlets, maps, photographs, Indian artifacts, pottery, Indian baskets, and assorted props all pertaining to the old and modern West."

In the early spring of 1970 another exhibition was planned in cooperation with Alys Freeze, head of the Western History Department of the Denver Public Library, to be held at the library, in the Western Room.

The National Broadcasting System in January of 1970 had presented a fifty-minute documentary on Charlie Russell narrated by Milburn

Stone ("Doc Adams" on the *Gunsmoke* television series). Using the "still pictures in motion" technique, the Russell paintings came to life on TV screens throughout the country. NBC made this film available to the library and it was shown numerous times during the Rosenstock Russell exhibition, which opened on May 16 and continued until June 13, 1970. The showing included three Russell oils, twenty-two watercolors, two pen and ink drawings, eight bronzes, and Russell letters embellished with his original drawings.

From time to time Fred would consider selling his Russell collection. By 1965 he had accumulated not only a substantial number of paintings, but also some valuable bronzes as well as books, articles, special brochures relating to the Montana artist; letters, many illustrated in color; various items inscribed by Russell in his own handwriting and often illustrated, such as programs and other ephemera. Not only did Fred feel that the collection should be made more accessible, but the cost of adequate insurance coverage had become so great that only an institution or a very wealthy individual could afford to maintain such a valuable galaxy.

In 1965 Brigham Young University indicated a strong interest, but the necessary funding was not available. For almost four years Fred held his collection intact while continuing his negotiations with the University, feeling quite strongly that the Russell materials should be retained as a unit. Unfortunately Brigham Young was unable to obtain the necessary funds, and Fred was forced to look in other directions. There were several groups and organizations—including the Denver Public Library — who were eager to have the Russell collection remain in Denver, but again the required funds were not available. During this period Fred had numerous opportunities to sell individual items or portions at a substantial profit, all of which he refused.

By the end of the sixties almost a half-century had passed since the day, his second in Denver, that he had enjoyed a steak dinner at Watrous's restaurant and vowed that one day he would own the large oil painting he had observed on the wall. Incidentally, some years later, reading that Mr. Watrous had died and that the restaurant was being closed, he contacted his widow and eventually purchased it. "I have had many fine paintings in my life — both as a collector and a dealer — but this one is still with me," Fred wrote in 1973. The painting depicted a scene during the Indian wars of the Custer period and the artist was J. Howard Martin.

Fred had been one of the early collectors of Western art, before the wave of nostalgia began its sweep across the country and the great American public joined the scholars in appreciating the heritage of the Frontier West and began seeking mementos, memorabilia, ephemera of the period, pilfering the trash dumps of old ghost towns, or in rare book-stores, or art museums. Accompanying this resurgence of interest in Western Americana was a sudden flourish of exhibitions. Norman Feder of Denver organized an exhibit, "Two Hundred Years of North American Indian Art," at the Whitney Museum of American Art in New York in 1971. One of the largest — which was a year-long traveling exhibition — was "The American West," originating at the Los Angeles County Museum of Art on March 21, 1972, then moving to the M. H. de Young Memorial Museum in San Francisco, and ending at the St. Louis Art Museum.

During its showing in Los Angeles a newspaper correspondent wrote, "While smog pollutes our atmosphere and industrial waste fouls our waters, citizens here are enjoying a robust exercise in ecological nostalgia at the Los Angeles County Museum of Art. A big exhibition called 'The American West,' it celebrates the days when rivers ran clean, the air was fresh and the vast open spaces of the West helped shape our dream of the country's limitless potential. . . .

"The artists of 'The American West' — among them Karl Bodmer, Alfred Jacob Miller, George Catlin, Seth Eastman, George Caleb Bingham, Carl Wimar, Worthington Whittredge, Albert Bierstadt, Thomas Moran, Charles M. Russell and Frederic Remington — were hardy souls, nearly all Europeans or Easterners, who ventured out alone or with exploring parties to report on the advancing frontier. Apart from

their esthetic achievements . . . they succeeded in compiling a magnificent pictorial record of the Western territories . . ."*

It was this urge by the populace to find refuge in the past, not only
to admire the West in a gallery but to own a piece of it — a book, a
manuscript, an artifact, a painting — that enhanced the collections that
Fred had acquired, increasing in value as each day passed.

But as the decades between 1920 and 1969 had been a time of acquisition, it appeared that the seventies would be a period of disbursement,
of relinquishing old and dear friends, both animate and inanimate.

*Grace Glueck, in *The New York Times*.

CHAPTER XV

THE GOLDEN YEARS

———— ∞∞∞∞∞ ————

"AS A BOOKMAN he specialized in literary first editions, schoolbooks, selected books of general interest, and Western Americana. He was able to locate through great personal effort and diligence, original diaries and manuscript collections of considerable historical significance and interest. His desire to have the contents of these historical treasures made more widely available led him into the publishing business. . . . His Old West Publishing Company has become a trademark for interesting source materials relating to the history of the West, as well as for fine workmanship in printing, illustrating, and binding. Mr. Rosenstock himself has, through personal drive and study, become a nationally recognized scholar in the field of Western Americana.

"Two of his productions have received particular national acclaim for scholarly research and fine printing: *Life in the Rocky Mountains,* a diary by Warren Ferris, edited by Paul C. Phillips; and *The West of William H. Ashley,* by Dale Morgan. In all these efforts, Mr. Rosenstock's wife, Frances, has always been by his side, a full partner in his business and collecting ventures as well as in their home with their family.

"Fred Rosenstock has assisted hundreds of Western historians and authors in their attempts to secure authentic information and background data to help them describe and accurately convey the spirit of the West. In this, he has struck up a strong personal identification with the growth, development, and activities of Brigham Young University and its fine library. Over the years many choice items have been guided by

Mr. Rosenstock to the University, where he sensed special interest sufficient to profit from his careful collecting efforts.

"Mr. President, in recognition of his expertise in the book world and for his significant contributions to the historical record of Western America — all of which have been instrumental in the favorable development of the Brigham Young University library — I recommend that Fred Asher Rosenstock be awarded the degree of Doctor of Humanities, *honoris causa.*"*

Fred received this singular honor on May 28, 1971, a remarkable accomplishment for an immigrant Jewish youth from Biala Potok, Austria, his childhood one of poverty, and whose formal education was aborted in high school. And this was only one of many plaudits.

In 1965, at an open house at the BYU library honoring the Rosenstocks, a statement was read to the gathering: "Because of the work of Fred and Frances Rosenstock our library now possesses some unusual resources among which is a strong collection of Western Americana with many scarce to rare items that highlight and enrich the collection's research potential; an interesting collection of the American theater; a very fine collection of books by and about Herman Melville . . . ; and a particularly rich collection of letters, autographs, and first editions of American and English literary authors, including many inscribed and presentation copies.

"In addition to making collections such as those noted above available to the library for purchase, the Rosenstocks have from time to time enriched our holdings by significant gifts. Among these are two oil paintings on Western themes by noted Colorado artists, Howland and Lillywhite, a pair of etchings by the noted Western artist, Ed Borein; a first edition of the very rare *Book of Commandments.*

"Their most recent gift is a manuscript account of Utah-Mormon interest, and also a very interesting journal of a trip from Iowa via Council Bluffs to the newly discovered gold fields in Bannack City, Montana, in the year 1864. . . .

*From the presentation made by Donald K. Nelson, Director of Libraries, BYU.

"Acquisitions and gifts such as these add real stature to a research collection, and we are particularly grateful to the Rosenstocks for their continuing interest in the growth of the library."

In 1970, Fred was selected as one of four judges at the exhibition of the work of Cowboy Artists of America held at the National Cowboy Hall of Fame in Oklahoma City, serving with Senator Barry Goldwater, Harold McCracken, and Robert Rockwell, prominent Western art collector from Corning, New York. In recognition of his work as a publisher, he was the recipient of the Award of Merit from the American Association for State and Local History and in 1970 was invited to serve on the Advisory Board of the Western History Center at the University of Utah.

Fred was a charter member of the Denver Posse of the Westerners, serving one term as Sheriff, and played an important role in the Western History Association, chairing one session on Western book publishing involving an illustrious panel of experts, including Alfred A. Knopf. His talents as a storyteller, as well as his knowledge of Western Americana, resulted in his being invited to speak at dozens of historical association meetings, libraries, and various other groups with Western interests.

Fred turned seventy-six in 1971, and although he wrote at that time, "My interest and enthusiasm are still at peakpoint," he was anxiously attempting to dispose of the Russell collection which had become both a financial and mental burden. By that time it had become apparent that the sale to Brigham Young University was not possible, and as his wife's health continued to deteriorate he concluded that he would have to sell his Russell materials at auction.

He began negotiations with Sotheby Parke Bernet, Inc., of New York, and it was eventually agreed that the sale would take place on October 19, 1972. Both Frances and Fred were relieved once the negotiations were completed, but it was difficult for Fred to engender much enthusiasm, realizing the terminal nature of his wife's illness. She had tried to rest up in Florida earlier in the year, later visited with Marilyn,

Jurors for the Fifth Annual Cowboy Artists of America Exhibition, from right: U.S. Senator Barry Goldwater; Dr. Harold McCracken; Fred Rosenstock; Robert Rockwell

her husband John, and the grandchildren in California. She spent some time at Palm Springs, but ultimately she decided that she would prefer to return to Denver. In July of 1972 she entered St. Joseph's Hospital, and died on July 31. It was Fred Rosenstock's most tragic moment.

Fortunately, with the auction scheduled a few months hence, Fred was busy preparing for the sale, working with James Maroney, Jr., on the assembling of the catalog and arranging for the shipping of the Russell materials to New York while continuing to operate the store.

The catalog was a masterpiece, including twenty-two full-color plates in its 124 pages, listing 73 entries covering dozens of individual Russell items. By 1975, the catalog itself had become a collector's item valued at forty to fifty dollars. Maroney, in his introduction, notes that "Fred Rosenstock has been a major figure in the world of Western history and literature . . . and an avid collector of both the written and artistic works of Charles M. Russell for over forty years. His enthusiasm and knowledge of American Western heritage has been generously shared with collectors, librarians, and scholars throughout the country. . . . At the age of seventy-seven, Mr. Rosenstock still owns and operates his bookstore in Denver which houses one of the most immense and impressive collections of Western Americana in private hands. . . ."

For the student of Russell, the catalog provided a provocative insight into the artist's character as well as a cross-section of his artistic life. And the nature of the items represented also indicated the perceptiveness of the collector in discovering and obtaining not "Russells for Russells' sake," but material that presented the man in all his facets.

What a tremendous book autograph party could have been staged with Charlie Russell doing the autographing. In a special presentation copy of Francis Parkman's *The Oregon Trail* Russell not only inscribed it, "To Mr. and Mrs. Howard Vanderslice With best whishes [*sic*] from C. M. Russell," but also painted watercolors at the beginning and end of eleven of the chapters. The collection being offered at auction also included a considerable number of Russell's interesting letters, filled with Russell humor and illustrated with black and white or color sketches.

One of the letters that has become a treasure was to Ted Abbott, written from Hollywood: "Frend Ted, . . . It takes sevral kinds to make a hero on the screen the beautiful Cow boy that makes love till the reformers want to burn the picture houses aint the same man that spures his horse of a thirty foot rim rock into the water and swims three miles to save his sweet hart from a band of out laws . . . this feller that goes of the rim rock is what they call a double Som actores donte use them some can ride as good as they make love. . . ." More than half of the first page of the letter is devoted to a color drawing of the star's "double" going "of a thirty foot rim rock into the water."

In addition to the books, letters, and ephemera, the sale included three pen and ink drawings, nine bronzes, and twenty-six paintings and watercolors, of which three were oils. Some were classic Russells: "Old Dad Lane and 'Mormon' Murphy riding with three pack horses through the snowy plains of Montana, a Nez Perce brave on an Appaloosa rides between them, killing Murphy;" and "Laughed at for his foolishness and shot dead by Slade" (Slade, pistol smoking, stands before his victim, who is crumbling at his feet); a Russell self portrait in watercolor; *The Challenge* (an intruding stallion challenging the territory of another, with the herd in the background observing the fight); *When the Trail Was Long Between Camps* (Indian women on horseback with their papooses and small children, drawing travois through a grassy plain); *Keeoma* (standing, full-length figure of an Indian maiden dressed in a colorful robe and with strands of beads about her neck); *The Buffalo Hunt* (five mounted Indians in chase of a buffalo herd on a grassy plain); and the masterpiece, *Captain Lewis Meeting the Shoshones* (midst a group from the expedition and several mounted Shoshones, Captain Lewis embracing a Shoshone chief).

Fred's previous experiences at selling (or buying) at auction had never been particularly successful, and the Sotheby Parke Bernet sale was no exception. A comparison made after the auction between the prices received in October 1972 and evaluations made of the collection in 1966 by Dr. Harold McCracken, Director of the Whitney Gallery of

Western Art and an expert on Russell, and Fred Rosenstock himself, revealed that most items were purchased at or near 1966 prices. Bidding was good for the less valuable to middle range items, but not good for the most valuable watercolors and oils. An example of the "bargain" prices: one Russell sold for $13,000 at the sale brought an offer one year later of $20,000 and was resold in the spring of 1974 for $22,500.

It was unfortunate that the Rosenstock Russell Collection could not have been purchased by a library, museum, or other institution where the items could have been more generally available and on public display. Throughout his career Fred attempted, whenever possible, to make his own interests subservient to the broader interests of the student of Western Americana.

An example of Fred's attitude relates to Andrew Drips, mentioned in the Ferris book as one of the men involved in the fur trade during the 1830–1835 period. 'A few years ago I got a letter from a Mrs. Hershey asking about my book, *Life in the Rocky Mountains,* then long out of print. She said she would like a copy because her grandfather was mentioned in it. I asked her who her grandfather was and it turned out to be Andrew Drips. After a further exchange, I learned that Mrs. Hershey had a number of Andrew Drips letters kept in a trunk he had carried with him in the mountains.

"By arrangement, Mrs. Hershey brought the Drips material to the Mayflower Hotel when I was on a trip to Los Angeles. She came with this little trunk filled with correspondence that involved the mountain men. We began looking at the letters and laying them out all over the room. I was so interested that she offered to leave it all with me that night and the next day. When she returned I asked what she planned to do with the material. She didn't want to sell the papers, and inquired about a worthy depository for them.

"It seemed to me this would fit well among the important collections in the Bancroft Library (University of California at Berkeley). I told her about that institution, and the manner in which the papers would be utilized for research by students, faculty, and other scholars. Mrs. Her-

the dark shadows of the rocks and pines, I stepped out
into the light, and walking along the sunny verge of a
precipice, seated myself on its extreme point. Looking
between the mountain-peaks to the westward, the pale-
blue prairie was stretching to the farthest horizon, like a
serene and tranquil ocean. The surrounding mountains
were in themselves sufficiently striking and impressive,
but this contrast gave redoubled effect to their stern
features.

Presentation copy of The Oregon Trail *with Russell watercolor*
Courtesy Sam Weller, Salt Lake City, Utah, and Sotheby Parke Bernet, Inc.

shey asked if I would take the material with me, and *give* it to the Bancroft Library. Remember, she had only met me the previous day.

"Two days later I marched into George Hammond's office (then Director of the Bancroft Library) and plunked the odd little trunk down on his desk. When he glimpsed the contents he became very excited and called in other members of his staff and the faculty to see it. They immediately wrote a letter of thanks to Mrs. Hershey and later had a reception in her honor."

In a letter to Fred, George Hammond wrote, "You will be pleased to know that I have received a letter from Mrs. Hershey, with regard to the Drips letters, acknowledging her pleasure that these have come to the Bancroft Library and your assistance in making the original suggestion. We are greatly indebted to you for your wonderful friendship and help."

Fred also made substantial contributions to a multitude of institutions in the West, some of which had great sentimental value, outweighing in many cases their monetary worth. On the occasion of one such donation, Lyman Tyler wrote, "Recently I read in *The Denver Post* of your gift to the Denver Museum of Natural History of certain items once owned by Captain William Clark: the dueling pistols, the powder flask, the glass telescope, and the codicil to Captain Clark's will. In addition to these personal items the gift also included the now scarce set of Thwaites's *Original Journals of the Lewis and Clark Expedition.*

"Reading the article . . . reminded me of the times I have seen these items in your home . . . I will always remember your showing these with pride, and explaining that the telescope was actually carried and used by Captain Clark on the renowned expedition of 1804 and 1806. You explained how these were kept in the Clark family and acquired by you through a great-grandson.

"Going to your home and seeing such items, along with your fine personal collection of rare books, letters and other manuscripts of famous literary and historical personalities, and your outstanding collection of Western art, was always something like combining visits to a great library, a museum, and an art gallery in one stop.

"You are to be complimented on your gift. . . . It is appropriate that these items . . . should stay in Denver, which has been your home and your place of business for almost fifty years. Also, Denver is truly a 'Western' town. These items . . . have found a fitting home."

To give some indication of the value of the gift, a pair of derringers said to have been owned by William F. Cody (who was on the scene seventy years after Lewis and Clark) were valued at $8,500 by Sotheby Parke Bernet.

In memory of his wife, Frances, Fred donated a Russell oil to the Denver Art Museum in 1973. The Museum acknowledged the gift in their publication, with this description: *"Standing Fearlessly, His Arms Thrown Downward Exposing His Breast,* was painted by Russell for use in *Sports Afield* (January, 1898) as an illustration for 'The Medicine Arrow,' a legend recounted by Anna P. Nelson.

"The story tells of an Indian youth whose 'trail was shadowed by evil fortune.' In an attempt to change his 'medicine,' he visits the Big Chief Mountain, where a tribe of 'wise little people' live who can help him. There he meets the White Owl who gives him a 'medicine arrow' with which to shoot the wild otter, whose skin he must wear in his hair. After he had carried out these instructions, 'the Sun shone in the young man's heart' and his skill at hunting became proverbial."

There are few institutions in the West, if they are at all involved with the history of America's frontier, that do not have some books, paintings, manuscripts, artifacts originally discovered or collected by Fred Rosenstock — be it the Bancroft Library, the University of Utah, Brigham Young University, the University of Arizona, the Denver Museum of Natural History, the Denver Art Museum, University of Wyoming, or the Western History Department of the Denver Public Library. Perhaps no other man in the West has more "living memorials" attesting to his achievements.

In 1975, having passed his eightieth birthday, and sorely missing his wife who was a vital part of his life for forty-six years, Fred Rosenstock, many of his friends believed, would — like old soldiers — fade away.

Shortly after Frances's death, and after he had auctioned off his Russell Collection, he talked frequently of disposing of his business. There were times when his shoulders slouched more than usual, and the character- istic sparkle was gone from his eyes. He had many vivid dreams of Frances, perhaps a subconscious fulfillment of a wish to be with her in some ethereal book hunter's paradise.

But these were only momentary periods of depression, soon replaced by a feeling of elation with another discovery of a first edition or another Russell painting. By the summer of 1975, however, he had entered into negotiations for the sale of his entire inventory, including his paintings and his collection of books and art at his home. Before the end of 1975, that vital institution of Western history, "Fred Rosenstock, Books and Art," had closed its doors, leaving a void that will probably never be filled.

Fred Rosenstock did not look back. With the same infectious smile and the sparkle back in his eyes, he was already planning, before the stock had been moved out of his store, for his new adventure. "I'm going to start an art gallery, and perhaps handle a few art books, and some Navajo rugs and Indian artifacts."

In a moment of reflection, Fred recalled that "Frances felt all her life that I devoted too much time to my work, but I would get into these books, or publishing, or art interests and would forget everything else. . . . I was so intense about what I was doing that I simply lost myself in it. But why did I do it? I can't tell you, except that I found myself in that element and loved it so much. But I don't think that was the moti- vation. I didn't have to do it *that* strong or go into it *that* deep.

"In my youth we really lived in poverty. My father and mother scraped in every way to make things go, even for food. I sold newspapers to help. I guess I acquired a sort of inherent feeling of the 'wolf at the door,' and the trouble was that even after I had chased the wolf away I couldn't stop. Because I came out of very humble circumstances, I also had a drive to succeed, to show people.

"This isn't a matter of bragging. When I gave that talk to the Western History Association in Salt Lake City, in 1963 — the time I introduced Alfred A. Knopf and other publishing notables — I spoke of the matter of historical writers striving for excellence. I was also referring to myself. I wanted to put in my own best effort. I wanted to be successful. To a certain extent, I will be frank, I wanted to prove this not only to myself, but to Frances, to everyone who knew me. But I overdid it. One reason, of course, was that I loved what I was doing, and it's a part of my nature to do things fully, with vigor, which is why I haven't always been too considerate of poor effort on the part of other people."

Perhaps it was the many nights he had spent sleeping on the countertop in the Bargain Book Store surrounded by thousands of books, or perhaps it was his total involvement in book collecting that engendered his many strange dreams. "I dream," he says, "of these things I once had. In fact, I dream of still having them. I have a dream library. It comes back to me, and it's housed in a certain way. It's in the attic of a house with sloping ceilings, and I even know some of the books that are in that library. They seem to be the same books all the time, in the same places and in the same bindings. Once or twice it has happened in my life that I quoted a book out of that dream library. And then I began to look for it. And once I definitely stated to somebody, 'I have that book, and it's bound in calf, and it's a nice copy.' Then I finally realized it was in my dream library."

An axiom among bibliophiles is that if you are a true collector, you cannot be a successful dealer. Fred was a rare exception. "Yes, I can truthfully, honestly, openly say that I am a collector. I'm even more than that — I'm a book enthusiast, but not a bibliomaniac, because that doesn't necessarily imply an interest in history, in the content. A bibliomaniac is pictured as a man bent over with a heavy pair of glasses, half-blind from reading too many books. And he's hunting around under the ceiling and among dusty books on the floor — he's a man who brings home a book with a feeling of greed. I can truthfully and happily say that I've been interested in books for what they are and for what they contain.

"There have been moments in my life when, if I had not had the books to give me happy feelings and happy times, then life would have been very dull indeed. It kept me at a high voltage point, and I have had many depressing things happen to me. It has been my great love of history and my great love of books, manuscripts, and diaries that has sustained me in my life. It has kept my enthusiasm high, and I believe I am a relatively younger man in spite of my advanced years because of these interests. And of course, remember that when you are a reader of history you are interested in current history that goes on from day to day as well. All of this is just a continuation of the feeling of enthusiasm for life that I've always had."

Before he had taken any definite steps toward disposing of his business, he said, "With the short time I have left, I should like to see my family in California more. So my thoughts are that I would like to get out of the book business . . . but I want to keep active in the thing that would require the least amount of time and space, so I would like to stay in art.

"Also, I would like to get away from living in a large house by myself. The only reason I have the house is because my private library is there. I am happy to be surrounded by my books, but the inconveniences of living alone in the house outweigh the pleasures. I would like to sell not only my stock of books at the store, but my private library. . . . Then I would like to move into a downtown hotel in Denver. I would like to have a study where I could show my paintings. I might have a couple of rooms with proper lighting, and show my art by appointment. I would not be completely out of books, because on my travels even without looking for such a thing, if I ran into something I would still contrive to acquire it. . . .

"I want to travel a little. I don't want to be tied to people. I want to exercise some liberty and choice of how to spend my time instead of being tied down day after day."

Fifty years from now, or a hundred, a young author will be searching the stacks at Bancroft, or Brigham Young University, or avidly fingering unpublished manuscripts at the Western History Department of the Denver Public Library, and he will note the name on the endpapers or scrawled in the corner of a manuscript, "Fred Rosenstock, Books." And then he will proceed to make his notes for a new project on Western Americana.

In the words of Fred Asher Rosenstock, "I think I can still continue to perform a service for the good of Western history, and I would want to continue it. I will never be at the point where I am not doing something for someone."

Fred Rosenstock is quite a prophet.

APPENDIX A

Selected Items from *1931 Americana* Catalog
issued by Fred A. Rosenstock

From the fly-leaf:

"This Catalogue of Americana from Denver is issued as the result of acquirement of several private collections. With the current active interest in the pioneer history of our Country, it should meet a ready response.

"Each item is in excellent condition, unless otherwise described. Prices are net, and do not include carriage. All orders are subject to prior sale, and those accompanied by remittance will receive first consideration."

8. BIGELOW, John. Memoir of the Life and Public Services of John Charles Fremont. Cl., 12mo., illus., N.Y., 1856. First Edition $2.00
   A good life of the "Pathfinder."

13. HORN, Tom. Life of Tom Horn, Government Scout and Interpreter, Written by Himself; Together with his Letters and Statements by His Friends; A Vindication. Wrappers, 12mo., illus., Privately Printed, Denver. (1904). $4.75
   Tom Horn was a capable government scout in his earlier days, but later he developed into a paid killer for Wyoming cattle interests.

30. REDPATH, James. The Public Life of Capt. John Brown. 12mo., Cl., Portrait, Boston, 1860. End-paper missing at front and back; otherwise good. $2.00

39. DAVIS, William Heath. Seventy-five Years in California. A History of Events and Life in California: Personal, political and Military; under the Mexican Regime; during the Quasi-Military Government of the Territory by the United States, and After the Admission of the State to the Union. Cl., 4vo., illus., maps, San Francisco, 1929 (John Howell). $10.00
   An elaborate and interesting volume on California from the Days of '49 on.

49–A. McCOY, Joseph G. Historic Sketches of the Cattle Trade of the West and Southwest. Cl., 8vo., illus., Kansas City, 1874. Nice copy. $60.00
   A view of the cattle business by an old cowman. Undoubtedly the best book ever written on its subject. Much on Texas and the Southwest; but the more

northern states of Kansas, Colorado, and Wyoming are also given a good share of the book. A rare item, steadily advancing in value.

56. DAVIS, Jefferson. The Rise and Fall of the Confederate Government. 2 vols., 8vo., ¾ morocco; N.Y., 1881. $7.50

The first edition of this famous history, by the President of the Confederacy.

70. JONES, J. B. A Rebel War Clerk's Diary at the Confederate States Capital. 2 volumes, 12mo., Cl., Phila., 1866. With autograph letter, appended, from Custis P. Jones, son of the "war clerk," referring to his father. $35.00

Nice set of this scarce work; a day-by-day diary of the most intimate character, with interesting comments as to events and occurrences "behind the lines" at the headquarters of the Confederate Government.

90. STEPHENS, Alex. H. The War Between the States. Thick 8vo., sheep, many illustrations. Title-page unfortunately missing, but fair copy otherwise. $2.25

91. TAYLOR, Richard. Destruction and Reconstruction: Personal Experiences of the Late War. 8vo., Cl., N.Y., 1879. $3.00

An interesting account, by a former Lieutenant-General in the Confederate Army.

94. WELLES, The Diary of Gideon; Secretary of the Navy under Lincoln and Johnson, 1861–1869. 3 vols., thick 8vo. Cloth; illus., Boston, 1911. First Edition. $15.00

A set, in mint condition, of this great work; an almost day-by-day Diary of Proceedings in the Cabinet during these Important Years.

108. BIRD, Isabella L. A Lady's Life in the Rocky Mountains. Cl., 12mo., illus., N.Y., 1879–80. $2.00

California, Colorado, especially full account of Estes Park, Colo.

113. CUSHMAN, Samuel & Waterman, J.P. The Gold Mines of Gilpin County, Colorado; Historical, Descriptive and Statistical. Cl., 12mo., Central City, 1876. $3.50

Besides the interesting text, there are many curious contemporary advertisements.

117. Colorado Directory & Gazetteer. The Rocky Mountain Directory and Colorado Gazetteer for 1871. Cl., 8vo., Denver, n.d., (1870). $7.50

Contains a brief history of Colorado; directories of Denver, Golden, Black Hawk, Greeley, etc.

123. COOK, John W. Hands Up; or Thirty-five years of Detective Life in the Mountains and on the Plains. . . . A Condensed Criminal History of the Far West. Cl., 8vo., illus., Denver, 1897. $10.00

The standard work of its kind on the Central Far West.

124. CORBETT, Thomas B. The Colorado Directory of Mines, containing a Description of the Mines and Mills and the Mining and Milling Corporations of Colorado . . . and a history of Colorado from its Early Settlement to the Present Time. Cl., 8vo., Denver, 1879. $4.50

First Edition of an important early mining book.

143. HALL, Frank. History of the State of Colorado . . . from 1858 to 1890. Full Morocco. 4to., Illus., Chicago, 1889. 4 vols. $7.50

One of the earliest and best complete histories of Colorado. This set has an auction record of $37.50.

161. POWELL, John W. Exploration of the Colorado River of the West and its Tributaries, explored in 1869, 1870, 1871 and 1872, under the Direction of the Secretary of the Smithsonian Institution. Cl., 4to., illus., maps, (sections). Washington. 1875. $7.00

A complete history of the famous Powell expedition which explored the Grand Canyon and the Colorado River in boats.

166. SCAMEHORN, G. N. Behind the Scenes, or Denver by Gas Light. Wrappers, 8vo., illus., Denver, 1894. $10.00

The Seamy side of early Denver; Gambling; Wolfe Londoner's election; Shooting of Nellie Ryan; Lynching of Dan Arata; Opium Joints; Robberies; Murders; Suicides. Scarce.

171. SMILEY, Jerome C. History of Denver, with Outlines of the Earlier History of the Rocky Mountain Country. Cl., 4to., illus., maps, Denver, 1903. $18.00

Special Autograph edition signed by the author, limited to 850 copies. A complete and good history of Colorado and Denver; not a mere compilation.

191. ROBINSON, Doane. History of South Dakota; together with mention of Citizens of South Dakota. Half Leather, 4to., Illus., Plans, n.p. 1904. 2 vols. $6.00

A history of South Dakota by a former president of the S. D. Historical Society and a very competent historian. Vol. 2 is composed entirely of biographical sketches and portraits.

193. FISKE, John. The Discovery of America, with some Account of Ancient America and the Spanish Conquest. The Large paper Edition, limited to 250

numbered sets. 4 vols., boards (½ cloth); illus., maps, Cambridge, 1892. $17.50

Beautifully printed on hand-made paper, this set is a joy to handle and read.

198. MULLAN, Captain John. Miners' and Travelers' Guide to Oregon, Washington, Idaho, Montana, Wyoming, and Colorado . . . Cl., 12mo., tab., Fold. Map., N.Y., 1865. $10.00

Recommendations for travelers, advice to emigrants by this route, Indians along the Route, Geography, Topography, etc.

215. CATLIN, George. North American Indians; being Letters and Notes on Their Manners, Customs and Conditions, Written During Eight Years Travel Amongst the Wildest Tribes of Indians in North America, 1832–1839. Two Vols. Cl., 8vo., Illus., (Colored) Maps. Edinburgh, 1926. New set, in jackets. $14.00

This Edinburgh, 1926, edition is the best Catlin with colored illustrations that has appeared in recent years.

240. REMINGTON, Frederic. Pony Tracks. Cl., 8vo., illus., N.Y., n.d. (1895). Mint copy. $3.50

A collection of Indian and hunting stories written and illustrated by Frederic Remington. Both stories and illustrations are exceptionally good.

264. CHITTENDEN, L. E. Recollections of President Lincoln and His Administration. 8vo., Cl., N.Y. 1891. A good Lincoln item; becoming scarce. $7.50

277. WHITNEY, Henry C. Life on the Circuit with Lincoln. Thick 8vo., Cl., Port., illustrations and facsimiles; Boston, n.d., (1892). $65.00

A fine copy of this rare book; classed with Herndon & Weik's Life as of first importance in dealing with the life of Lincoln, particularly his early life. A necessary key to any collection of Lincolniana.

296. BANVARD, John. Description of Banvard's Panorama of the Mississippi River, Painted on Three Miles of Canvas; exhibiting a View of Country, 1200 Miles in Length, extending from the Mouth of the Missouri River to the City of New Orleans; Being by Far the Largest Picture Ever Executed by Man. Wrappers, 8vo., Boston, 1847. $5.00

Biography of John Banvard and a description of his wonderful painting. Has a good deal of early history of the Lower Mississippi.

299. Montana Territory. History and Business Directory; Distances, Fares and Altitudes, Counties, Towns, Mining Camps; Commercial, Mineral and Agricultural Interests; With a Sketch of the Vigilantes. Helena, 1879; Fisk Bros.,

Printers and Binders. Cl., 8vo., Illus., Fold. Map, Tables. $10.00
  Compiled by F. F. Warner. Much on Vigilantes, First Discovery of Gold, etc.

305. LUMMIS, Charles F. The Enchanted Burro. Stories of New Mexico and
South America. Cl., 12mo., illus., Chicago, 1897. $2.50
  Tales of Peru, New Mexico, Bolivia.

307. New Mexico. An Illustrated History of New Mexico. Containing a History
of this Important Section of the Great Southwest from the earliest Period of its
Discovery to the Present Time; together with Glimpses of its Auspicious Future, Full Leather, 4to., ports., illus., maps, Chicago, 1895. $8.00
  Contains, besides portraits, many illustrations of churches, mines, etc. A few
pages slightly water stained, but on the whole a good copy.

320. ROCK, Marion Tuttle. Illustrated History of Oklahoma; its occupation
by Spain and France — its Sale to the United States — its Opening to Settlement in 1889 — and the Meeting of the First Territorial Legislature. Cl., 8vo.,
illus., Topeka, 1890. $7.50
  Guthrie, the Indians, Land Openings, Oklahoma City, Public Schools, the
Press, Bench and Bar, etc.

378. McCONNELL, H. H. Five Years a Cavalryman; or Sketches of Regular
Army Life on the Texas Frontier twenty years ago. Cl., 12mo., Jacksboro,
Texas, 1889. $6.50
  Indian fighting, etc. Printed on tinted paper. New copy.

407. AUDUBON, John W. Audubon's Western Journal; 1849–1850. Being the
Ms. record of a Trip from New York to Texas, and an Overland Journey
through Mexico and Arizona to the Gold Fields of California. Introduction,
notes and index by Frank Heywood Hodder. Cl., 8vo., illus., fold. map. Cleveland, 1906. $6.00
  Written by the son of the great naturalist, James J. Audubon.

429. FRENCH, Hon. William. Some Recollections of a Western Ranchman in
New Mexico, 1883–1899. Cl., 8vo., N.Y., n.d. $3.75
433. HAYDEN, F. V. Sun Pictures of Rocky Mountain Scenery; with a Description of the Geographical and Geological Features and Some Account of
the Resources of the Great West; containing 30 photographic views along the
line of the Pacific Railroad, from Omaha to Sacramento. Half Leather, (somewhat rubbed), 4to., illus., N.Y., 1870. $12.50
  These views are actual photographs bound in the book.

465. VIVIPAROUS QUADRUPEDS OF NORTH AMERICA by John James
Audubon, F.R.S., etc. and Rev. John Bachman, D.D., etc.

The Viviparous Quadrupeds of North America. First Edition. 150 plates in
2 volumes, folio, 21½ x 27½ inches; the text in 3 volumes, royal 8vo. Together,
5 volumes, half-russia, New York 1845-54. Both volumes of plates dated 1845
on title-page. The individual plates are dated from 1842 to 1848. The 3 volumes
of text are dated 1846, 1851, and 1854, respectively. Volume 3 of the text contains the 5 extra colored plates; making 155 plates in all.

While this work will not approach the value of the great folio edition of Audubon's Birds, it is, nevertheless, a set that is due for a great advance in price.
The original subscription price of this set in parts before binding, was $300.

Volume 2 of the text is somewhat water-stained; but, as a whole, this is a
good, sound set, with all of the plates in fine, clean condition.

Correspondence invited on this item.

Price $500.00

APPENDIX B

Selected Items from *1934 Americana* Catalog
issued by Fred A. Rosenstock including
A Personal Word from the Publisher

As a number of my good book-friends and clients know, I have 'threatened' to issue this, my second catalogue of Americana, for more than a year. Now that it is out, I have a somewhat naive expectancy as to how it may fare. Conditions in the rare-book field being still uncertain, it might have been more prudent to hold a little longer. Yet, I could not resist the desire to get these books and pamphlets in circulation; into the hands of collectors and libraries that need them more. Many of these rarities represent thrilling adventure in their acquisition; and the process of packing off some pamphlet to a person in Rhode Island will at once bring the thought, "I'd like to tell him how many times my heart was in my mouth coming down that slippery, wet, narrow mountain road that night, with the brakes 'on the blink', to Breckenridge and back; all for that pamphlet." In the spare West, where old families are few and distances far between, the hunt for rare books is more exciting even if more laborious; and thereby is some degree of compensation. Suffice to say, there are more than a few numbers in the catalogue that I never expect to find or own again.

If the catalogue has any measure of success, I shall be encouraged to issue another — smaller perhaps, but equally interesting — in the not too remote future. This would contain groups from two private collections of Americana to which I have but recently gained access; a smattering of important American literary rarities — first editions in their correct state; and as a special feature, two unusual original Lincoln letters written from Springfield, in 1845 and 1846.

As a parting thought, it has always been a fond wish to personally meet some of my clients with whom I have corresponded for years. Should any of you visit Denver, I invite you to look me up. My sincere thanks to all of you for past and future patronage.

Fred A. Rosenstock

The 1934 Catalogue, 84 pages, included over 1300 items. Those listed here are some of the more interesting, or more significant, not necessarily the most valuable or the most important.

BEADLE'S LIBRARY

16. Beadle performed a real service to American youth when he published these stories usually called "dime novels." Though overdrawn, they have a tang of the real thing about them. There is today, undoubtedly, an attitude of respect toward the Beadle thrillers; and they are fast being recognized as the mythology of the frontier, the outlaw, and the Indian killer. An unusual feature of the run of Beadles listed here is that they are in immaculate condition. Some numbers are, in fact, unopened.

[Following is a list of 34 individual titles, varying in price from $3.00 to $5.00.]

41. CROCKETT, David; Narrative of the Life of. Written by himself. 12mo. orig. cloth; paper label defective; first edition. Phila. 1834. A nice copy of this Crockett high-spot. $20.00

The preface says, "this is truly the very thing itself — the exact image of its author."

71. PIKE, Gen. Albert. Poems: with introductory biographical sketch by his daughter, Mrs. Lilian Pike Roome. 8vo., ¾ leather (binding somewhat worn and slightly warped); Little Rock, 1900. $6.00

Pike wrote the famous "Prose Sketches and Poems written in the western country," published in 1834. For many years he was head of the Scottish Rite Masons in this country. Several of the poems in this volume are on western subjects. Scarce.

93. BLEDSOE, A. J. Indian Wars of the Northwest. A California sketch. 8vo. cloth; 505 pp.; San Francisco, 1885. $27.50

The rare first edition with the errata slip at the top of page 9. Contains the annals of the party of Dr. Josiah Gregg in which that old western traveler met his death by starvation in northern California. Much on the Indians wars and trials and tribulations of the early settlers.

128. MANLY, William L. Death Valley in '49. 12mo. cloth; 498 pp., San Jose, Calif. 1894. $17.50

The autobiography of a pioneer of 1849; and particularly recites the sufferings of the band of men, women and children who gave "Death Valley" its name. A fine copy of the scarce first edition.

156. SIMPSON, Sir George. Peace River: a Canoe Voyage from Hudson's Bay to Pacific, in 1828. 8vo. orig. wrappers; 119 pp., map.; Ottawa, 1872. Rare. $45.00

Journal of the late chief factor, Archibald McDonald, (Hudson's Bay Company) who accompanied Simpson. Edited with notes by M. McLeod. This is the scarcest of all of Sir George Simpson's books. With slip of errata before title.

176. GORDON, Gen. John B. Reminiscences of the Civil War. 8vo. cloth; 474 pp.; N.Y., 1903. $5.00

By an important general of the Confederate army. A book much sought after.

227. BARNEY, Libeus. Early-day Letters from Auraria (now Denver); to the Bennington (Vermont) Banner. 8vo., original wrappers; 88 pp.; Denver, n.d.; rebacked; otherwise, a complete copy in all particulars. $75.00

One of the rarest of Denver books. Though published since 1900, it is almost as rare as Pike's Peak guides themselves. These letters, originally written in 1859 and 1860, give the very earliest information on the gold rush and first days in Denver city.

232. BLISS, Edward. A Brief History of the New Gold Regions of Colorado Territory; together with Hints and Suggestions to intending emigrants. 8vo. wrappers (new wrapper covers); printed by John W. Amerman, N.Y., 1864; 30 pp.; and map. Inscribed in the autograph of the author. $200.00

Bliss had been editor of the Rocky Mountain News. In its last sale at auction, in 1923, this pamphlet was described as "one of three known copies." A general description of Colorado; and refutes the "Great American Desert" idea. Gives a table of distances from Atchison, on the Missouri river, to Denver. Much important first-hand information on early Colorado. The map shows the stage-route across the "Buffalo country," and the gold regions west of Denver.

258. Creede, Colorado. Creede Camp; "the Greatest Mineral Discovery since the days of Leadville. Fourth Place already gained by the Young Giant." 8vo., orig. wrappers; 16 pp.; curious illustrations; no place, no date, (Denver, 1892). An excellent copy of this rare pamphlet on the Creede excitement. $35.00

Details of the mines, the town, the people, and "How to reach the promised land," Views of the gulch, and a map of the region. Although somewhat optimistic, it gives an excellent account of this important mining camp, of which little has been written.

263. CROFUTT, Geo. A. Grip-sack guide of Colorado. A Complete encyclo-

pedia of the State. Resources; where to hunt and fish; altitudes; distances, etc. 8vo. flexible cloth; original edition; 183 pp.; Omaha, 1881. $4.50

Issued as a guide for tours over the various railroads. Some history, and a fine folding map in colors.

270. Map of Denver, Auraria, and Highland; 28x22"; folding into 16mo. stamped cloth cover. Published by H. M. Fosdick and L. N. Tappan; Denver: Dec. 1, 1859. Scale 800 ft. to the inch. $90.00

The excessively rare FIRST map of Denver. The Historical Society of Colorado has this map, framed, included in their exhibition of rare Coloradoana. There are not more than three or four known to be in existence.

297. HOWBERT, Irving. The Indians of the Pike's Peak Region. Including an account of the battle of Sand Creek, and of occurrences in El Paso County, Colorado, during the war with the Cheyennes and Arapahoes, in 1864 and 1868. 8vo. cloth; 230 pp., N.Y., 1914. $10.00

An important contribution to the Indian war history of Colorado. Especially valuable for Sand Creek Massacre; in which Howbert took part as a member of Chivington's command.

301. UNRECORDED COLORADO RARITY. Laws of Independent District; revised and adopted February the 15th, A.D., 1861. 16mo. original wrappers; 12 pp., Denver: The Rocky Mountain News Printing Company, 1861. $275.00

Of first importance. One of the earliest district mining laws of the region; lying between Boulder and Clear Creek. Also, a rare, early Denver imprint. The laws themselves are not at all "dry." For instance, sec. 37, "Murder," states: "Any person found guilty of wilful murder shall be hanged by the neck till dead, and then given to his friends if called for, and if not, to be decently buried."

311. MATHEWS, A. E. (artist): Pencil Sketches of Colorado; its principal Towns and Scenery. Contains 22 pages of colored plates; being sketches drawn on the spot by the artist, of streets and scenery in Denver in the '60's; early views of Central City, Golden, and other parts of the state. The drawings are well-executed, and the coloring is brilliant and spirited. There are several pages of descriptive text at the back of the book. This extremely rare early view-book of Colorado has practically never come up for sale anywhere; and in Denver it is regarded as one of the most desirable pieces of Coloradoana. Separate plates from this book have fetched high prices. Oblong folio cloth; 13½" x 19¼"; lithographed and published by J. Bien, N.Y., 1866. This copy is in un-

usually good condition; all of plates being clean and complete. There are a number of library stamps throughout the book; generally on the reverse side of plates. This copy was once the property of a Colorado school library, from whom it was legitimately purchased. $300.00

EARLY AMERICAN PAPERBACK THRILLERS

396. The field of the early American popular novel has of late captivated the most virile interest of students of American literary history. Particularly absorbing is the subject of the old American "paper-back," of Civil War, and even earlier, vintage. Here is presented a unique run of novels — all except one in original wrappers and pictorial covers. The physical condition of most of the numbers is decidedly unusual; some actually being almost as fresh as when issued, seventy or eighty years ago, as the case may be. If for no other reason, they are desirable as curiosities of marvellous longevity of life of frail paper-covered booklets.

[Following is a list of 17 titles, varying in price from $2.50 to $5.00.]

511. DAWSON, T. F. and Skiff, F.J.V. The Ute War: a History of the White River Massacre and the Privations and Hardships of the Captive White Women among the Hostiles on Grand River. 8vo. original wrappers; perfect; Denver, 1879. $385.00

An almost pristine copy of this rare Indian massacre and captivity item. Universally regarded as one of the very rarest Colorado-published books. Not more than two or three copies have come up at auction; and the writer does not recall ever seeing it listed in a dealer's catalog of Americana. This was the famous incident in Colorado history, when the White River Utes killed N. C. Meeker, the agent of the reservation, and held members of his family captive.

723. TWITCHELL, Ralph Emerson. The Spanish Archives of New Mexico. 2 volumes; thick 8vo. cloth; as new; Cedar Rapids, 1914. $15.00

The early history of New Mexico is that of the Spanish invaders and settlers, and the student must turn to sources such as this to get at the truth. Many of the documents are printed in full (translated); and others less important are epitomized. Chronologically arranged with historical, genealogical, geographical and other annotations.

804. SMITH, Captain John. The True Travels, Adventures, and Observations; in Europe, Asia, Africa, and America, from 1593 to 1629. His sea-fights in the Straights; his Service in Hungaria, Transylvania, etc.; his combats with the

Turks and Tartars; together with a Continuation of his general History of Virginia, Summer-Isles, New England, and their proceedings, since 1624, to this present 1629; as also of the new Plantations of the great River of the Amazons. A beautiful copy of the rare first edition; imperial 8vo., 60 pages, tastefully bound in full blue crushed levant. London: Printed by J. H. for Thomas Slater, and are to be sold at the Blew Bible in Greene Arbour, 1630. The exquisite folding plate, illustrating various phases of Smith's adventurous career, has been skilfully mounted, to insure permanency. $385.00

859. Reports of Explorations and Surveys to ascertain the most practicable and economical Route for a Railroad from the Mississippi River to the Pacific Ocean. Made under direction of the Secretary of War in 1853-54. 13 volumes in 12; 4to.; profuse with illustrations and maps; Washington, 1855-60. $23.50

This famous set is rapidly growing scarce, especially in complete form. Particularly notable for the many magnificent colored views of western scenery; also the numerous plates of animals, birds, etc.

911. BAKER, Jim; The Life of; 1818–1898. Trapper; scout; guide, and Indian fighter. By Nolie Mumey. 8vo. boards; 234 pp.; map and illus.; new copy; Denver, 1931. $12.50

Baker was about the last of the real mountain men to pass on. One of 250 signed and numbered copies.

1119. Lewis and Clark. The Original Journals of the Lewis and Clark expedition, 1804–1806. Printed from the original manuscripts; together with manuscript material of Lewis and Clark and others now for the first time published in full and exactly as written. Edited, with introduction, notes and index by R. G. Thwaites. 8 volumes; 8vo. cloth; N.Y., 1904. $90.00

This is really the first edition of these journals; as all others, including the Biddle edition of 1814, are merely clever paraphrases of the journals as written by the explorers. Included here is a fine bibliography of Lewis and Clark books; also the journals of Floyd and Whitehouse. In the appendix are letters and records of the expedition; and the volume of maps is a facsimile reproduction of the maps drawn on the journey.

1319. MERCER, A. S. The Banditti of the Plains, or the Cattlemen's Invasion of Wyoming in 1892. "The crowning infamy of the ages." 8vo. cloth; 139 pp.; original edition; Cheyenne (1894). $115.00

A complete, though biased, account of the cattle war in Wyoming in 1892. A fair and impartial account appears in the recently-published *Malcolm Camp-*

bell, Sheriff. The present book was written at a time when the whole state was divided into factions, and this is a so-called "rustler's" version. However, there are many prominent names mentioned, and later versions do not not relieve these men of blame and wrong-doing. As in most wars, both sides lost more than they gained. A scarce and important book on western history. Brought $260 in Thomas sale.

APPENDIX C

Western Books Published by the Old West Publishing Company
(Listed in sequence of date of publication)

Ferris, Warren A. *Life in the Rocky Mountains; A Diary of Wanderings on the Sources of the Rivers Missouri, Columbia, and Colorado, 1830–35;* edited by Paul C. Phillips. 1940.[†]

Schoberlin, Melvin. *From Candles to Footlights; A Biography of the Pikes Peak Theatre, 1859–76.* History of the theatre in Colorado during its Territorial Period. 1941.[†]

Frink, Maurice. *Cow Country Cavalcade; 80 Years of the Wyoming Stock Growers Ass'n.* 1954.

Frink, Maurice; Jackson, Turrentine; Spring, Agnes Wright. *When Grass Was King.* Contributions to the Western Range Cattle Industry Study. 1956.[†]

Beckwourth, James Pierson. *Enigmatic Figure of the West.* His later years. Edited by Dr. Nolie Mumey. 1957.[†]

Ickis, Alonzo Ferdinand. *Bloody Trails Along the Rio Grande.* Diary and Biography of a Soldier in Company B of the Colorado Volunteers in the Civil War in the West. Edited by Dr. Nolie Mumey. 1958.[†]

Pritchard, James Avery. *The Overland Diary* of James Avery Pritchard from Kentucky to California in 1849. Edited by Dale L. Morgan. 1959.[†]

Mattes, Merrill. *Indians, Infants and Infantry; The Story of Major Andy Burt in Indian Fighting Days on the Northern Plains.* 1960.

Burt and Berthoud. *The Rocky Mountain Gold Regions (1861).* A First Reprint, with exhaustive revalatory introduction by James G. Hodgson. 1962.[†]

Doble, John. *John Doble's Journal and Letters from the Mines.* California gold rush. Edited by C. L. Camp. 1962.

Latham, Dr. Hiram. *Trans-Missouri Stock Raising.* 1st reprint (with additions) of rare original edition of 1871. Edited by J. C. Dykes. 1962.

Wyer, Malcolm Glenn. *Books and People.* Personal autobiographical sketches in the life of a noted librarian. 1964.[†]

Ashley, William H. *The West of William H. Ashley; Diaries and Letters of William H. Ashley & His Contemporaries.* Edited by Dale L. Morgan. 1964.

Draper, Benjamin. *Georgetown Pictorial.* Highlights in the history of an early Colorado silver mining town. 1964.

Mumey, Nolie. *Nathan Addison Baker,* Pioneer Journalist, Colorado, Wyoming. 1965.

White. Philo White's *Narrative of a Cruise in the Pacific to South America and California on the U.S. Sloop-of-War "Dale," 1841–43.* Edited by C. L. Camp. 1965.

Yount, George C. *George C. Yount and His Chronicles of the West.* Early Southwest and California from 1820's. Edited by C. L. Camp. 1966.

Coit, Daniel Wadsworth. *Digging for Gold Without a Shovel: Letters of Daniel Wadsworth Coit from Mexico & California, 1848–51.* Illustrated with his own sketches. Edited by George P. Hammond. 1967.

Becker, Robert H., Editor. *Thomas Christy's Road Across the Plains.* From Mormon Crossing on the Missouri to Sacramento. With unique cartography (a map for each day on the trail). 1969.

Hafen, Ann W. *Campfire Frontier.* Romantic biographical sketches and poems; adventuresome epics of the Old West. 1969.

Tyler, S. Lyman, editor. *The Montana Gold Rush Diary of Kate Dunlap.* Published in cooperation with University of Utah Press. 18 duotone reproductions. 1969.

Dillon, Richard H., editor. *A Cannoneer in Navajo Country; Journal of Private Josiah M. Rice, In Arizona, In 1851.* 22 sketches by diarist. 1970.

Todd, Edgeley W., Editor. *A Doctor on the California Trail: Diary of Dr. John Hudson Wayman from Indiana to the Gold Fields in 1852.* 1971.

Hafen, LeRoy R. *Broken Hand; The Life of Thomas Fitzpatrick, Mountain Man, Guide and Indian Agent.* Rewritten and expanded edition. 1973.

Hafen, LeRoy R. and Ann W. *The Joyous Journey.* An autobiography. Published in cooperation with the Arthur H. Clark Co., Glendale, Calif. 1973.

Hammond, George P. *The Adventures of Alexander Barclay, Mountain Man in Colorado and New Mexico and Builder of Barclay's Fort on the Santa Fe Trail in 1848.* 1976.

* Ferris, Warren A. *Life in the Rocky Mountains.* A new edition of this Fur

Trade classic, with recently discovered contributary material of significance. Edited by LeRoy Hafen.

* Simmons, Philander. *Man of the Early West*. Trapper, hunter, guide, prospector. Edited by Frederic E. Voelker.

* Burke, Joseph. *With the Fur Traders*. Account of a naturalist with the Brigades of the Hudson's Bay Company, 1843-1847. Edited by Lois Stone.

* Books in process in 1976.
† Out of print.

FRED ROSENSTOCK: *A Legend in Books and Art*
WAS DESIGNED BY PAUL WEAVER,
SET IN 14-POINT LINOTYPE GRANJON,
AND PRINTED ON MOUNTIE WARM WHITE TEXT.
BOUND BY ROSWELL BOOKBINDING, PHOENIX.